RE-IMAGINING ANIMATION

—

THE CHANGING FACE OF THE MOVING IMAGE

D0117316

—

PAUL WELLS
JOHNNY HARDSTAFF

An AVA Book
Published by
AVA Publishing SA
Rue des Fontenailles 16
Case Postale
1000 Lausanne 6
Switzerland
Tel: +41 786 005 109
Email: enquiries@avabooks.ch

Distributed by
Thames & Hudson
(ex-North America)
181a High Holborn
London WC1V 7QX
United Kingdom
Tel: +44 20 7845 5000
Fax: +44 20 7845 5055
Email:
sales@thameshudson.co.uk
www.thamesandhudson.com

Distributed in the USA
and Canada by:
Watson-Guptill Publications
770 Broadway
New York,
New York 10003 USA
Fax: +1 646 654 5487
Email:
info@watsonguptill.com
www.watsonguptill.com

English Language
Support Office
AVA Publishing (UK) Ltd.
Tel: +44 1903 204 455
Email:
enquiries@avabooks.co.uk

Design
Emmi Salonen
www.emmi.co.uk

Production
AVA Book Production
Pte. Ltd., Singapore
Tel: +65 6334 8173
Fax: +65 6259 9830
Email:
production@avabooks.com.sg

All reasonable attempts
have been made to trace,
clear and credit the
copyright holders of
the images reproduced
in this book. However,
if any credits have
been inadvertently
omitted, the publisher
will endeavour to
incorporate amendments
in future editions.

© AVA Publishing SA 2008

All rights reserved. No part
of this publication may be
reproduced, stored in a
retrieval system or
transmitted in any form or
by any means, electronic,
mechanical, photocopying,
recording or otherwise,
without permission of the
copyright holder.

ISBN 2-940373-69-8 and
978-2-940373-69-7

10 9 8 7 6 5 4 3 2 1

TR
897.5
.W46
2006

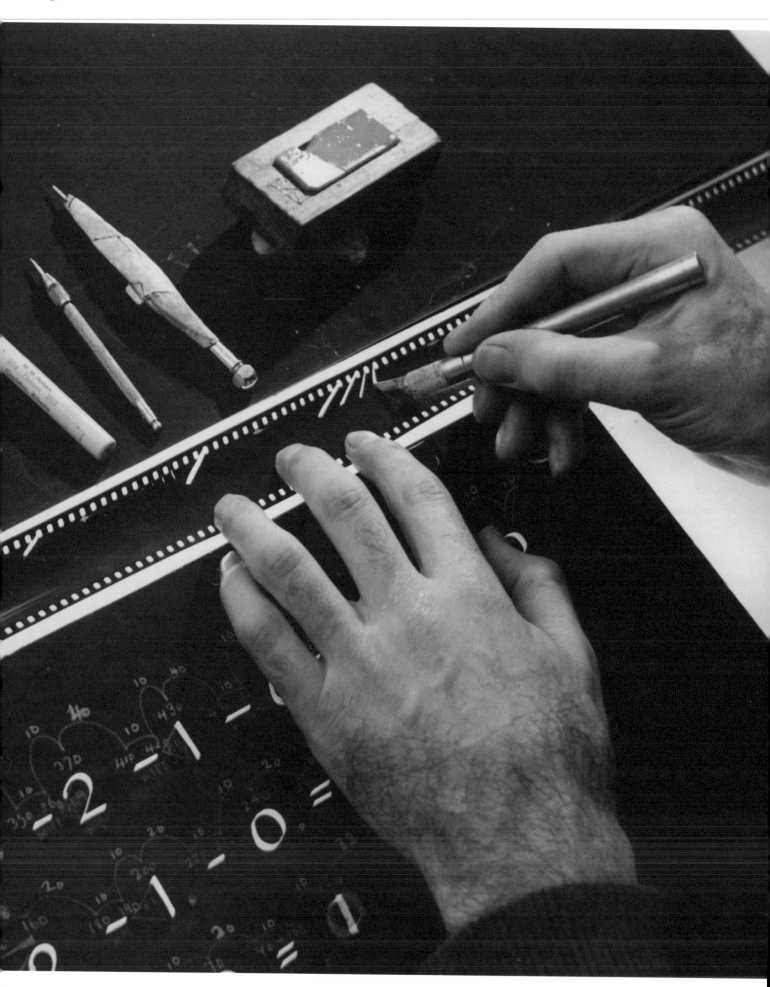

CONTENTS

—

—

01

—

02

—

03

— Front matter

— Contents
Introduction
How to get the most
out of this book

— 004/005

C

—

—

04

—

05

INTRODUCTION

—

In recent years, the 'digital revolution' has consolidated major changes in moving image practices, privileging the computer as not merely the facilitator of processes involved in creating moving image works, but generating moving images too. It is possible that we are closing in on the post-photographic era, where film will be viewed as an arcane medium of image generation. For many, this is already old news and their work takes for granted the application and assimilation of computer software and its attendant creative tools, which establish new forms of visualisation and pictorial effect.

One of the chief consequences of these developments is the elevation of animation as a core term of description for many aspects of creative image-making endeavours. This is mainly through the ways in which the intrinsic artifice and illusionism of traditional animation is seemingly embedded within, or directly echoes, the simulation and synaesthesia that now characterises contemporary film-making. This in turn has in some senses made 'animation' a redundant term – a mere catch-all that speaks to all manipulated moving-image practices. It is the intention of this book to address this issue and to delineate animation further through its specific applications and authorial intentions.

In the contemporary era, animation has been reabsorbed into debates about film-making in general. It is no longer considered a 'second cousin' to live action, or merely understood as 'the cartoon' or 'the experimental film'. Rather, it is now viewed as profoundly instrumental to film in general because of the digital animation interventions (visual effects) that are endemic to even the most mundane realist narratives and define the moving image palette. If animation was once understood as an adjunct of film and a backwater in cinema, it now finds itself as the core condition of film-making per se. In what is surely to become a seminal statement in defining this new model of digital live-action cinema, Lev Manovich concludes it is 'live action material + painting + image-processing + compositing + 2D computer animation + 3D computer animation', adding that:

—

'The manual construction of images in digital cinema represents a return to nineteenth century pre-cinematic practices, when images were hand-painted and hand-animated. At the turn of the twentieth century, cinema was to delegate these manual techniques to animation, and define itself as a recording medium. As cinema enters the digital age, these techniques are again becoming the commonplace in the film-making process. Consequently, cinema can no longer be clearly distinguished from animation.' [1]

—

Taiwanese artist Agi Chen brings together the worlds of the traditional cartoon, new media technology and arts culture by taking the colours used in a cartoon, rendering them in new geometric forms, and then re-embedding them in a scene from the original film.

Front matter   Contents
                 Introduction
                 How to get the most
                 out of this book

006/007

INTR

While this view correctly determines the historical status and technical influence of animation and its place within contemporary film-making, it remains insufficient on two counts. First, it merely defines animation within its parameters as a form co-opted by the computer and neglects to acknowledge the myriad forms of animation not made in this way. Secondly, and especially pertinent to this book, is that it also signals a sense of homogeneity in the way that animation has been absorbed by cinema, and seemingly does not declare its difference any longer.

It is clear, though, that animation can still signal difference in nominally traditional ways – through the cartoon, 3D stop motion, or even computer-generated imagery in the dominant Pixar-style aesthetic, and indeed, many other techniques and approaches. Further, it is a term with currency beyond the remit of the feature film and television programme. Animation is a vehicle that has come to delineate the possibilities available to moving image cultures in any style, context or technique and, perhaps most importantly, in a range of disciplines. As the previously assured processes and disciplines of image production collapse into one another, or irrevocably change, it is necessary to 're-imagine' animation.

Animation, under these conditions, has come to adopt its original meaning as the essential 'animus' at the heart of cross-disciplinary, interdisciplinary and multidisciplinary approaches to creating moving images. Film-makers may now be understood as 'animators' of their work without any sense that they animate in the traditional ways while, equally, if sometimes unconsciously and intuitively, working with the illusionist sensibility of the traditional animation auteur. Indeed, it is of critical importance to re-explore animation through the intentions of its creator and the contexts in which it is made. It is this, more than anything else, that re-defines and re-imagines animation as a state-of-the-art vehicle for moving image cultures.

This wider definition of animation affords the opportunity of testing its parameters and boundaries, in order to interrogate how the many and varied approaches to making film, graphics, visual artefacts, multimedia and other intimations of motion pictures can now be delineated and understood. **Re-imagining Animation** will address these issues through an engagement with a range of moving-image works, looking at the context in which they were produced; the approach to their preparation and construction; the process of their making; the critical agenda related to the research; developmental and applied aspects of the work; the moving-image outcomes; and the status of the work within contemporary art and design practices.

In recent years, consolidated ma practices, privile merely the facili creating moving moving images t closing in on the where film will medium of imag is already old ne granted the appl computer softw tools, which esta visualisation and

consequences of the elevation of of description fo image-making er through the way artifice and illusi animation is seen or directly echoe synaesthesia tha contemporary fil in some senses n term – a mere ca all manipulated r It is the intentior this issue and to further through i and authorial inte

animation has be about film-makin considered a 'sec merely understoc experimental film

These production processes will also be addressed through a variety of core critical perspectives, taking into account the presence and status of the works as they speak to and influence debates about arts education, ideology and aesthetics, technology and authorship, and contemporary moving-image culture. In an era when definitions of social, cultural and arts practices are unclear, subject to blurred disciplinary boundaries and predicated on uncertain ends and outcomes, it is important not merely to reframe the questions about how such practices should be defined, but to table a range of answers. This will be achieved through an understanding of the core processes of creative engagement and an address of animation as a versatile language that, to coin a phrase, can 'speak in many tongues'.

Re-imagining Animation will seek to identify this language, demonstrate and illustrate creative practice, and offer a variety of views as to why animation, from pencil to pixel, offers a radical and uninhibited outlook to moving image culture.

—

—

—

REFERENCES
1. Manovich, L. (2001)
   The Language of New Media,
   Cambridge & London:
   MIT Press

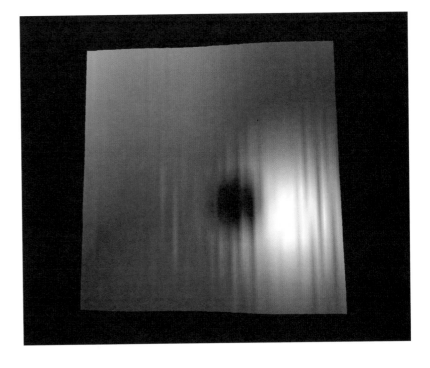

Front matter　　Contents
　　　　　　　　Introduction
　　　　　　　　How to get the most
　　　　　　　　out of this book

008/009

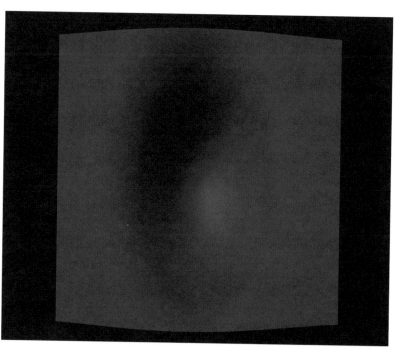

These moving image works
by artist Anne-Sarah Le Meur,
entitled **Eye-Ocean**, represent
the idea of 'generative art
work' - a piece that takes
place in silence and is of
infinite length. Two virtual
or 3D synthetic lights - a
black and a bright coloured
one - move, appear and
disappear, join and disjoin,
over a square animated
surface. The computer program
driving the piece controls
the visual parameters and
prompts other variations that
make the light phenomena
change in simple periodic
loops, generating continuous
minimalist, slow and sensual
infinite metamorphoses. Such
generative work is in essence
a form of animation,
especially given its central
condition of metamorphosis.
However, it is privileged
to a gallery space and
the agenda of art critics.

HOW TO GET
THE MOST OUT
OF THIS BOOK

The structure of the book offers different levels of information and interest. The main text privileges the voice of the authors, the words of the contributing artists, and provides the central argument of the book.

All images have accompanying captions, which attempt to add additional information and suggest further ideas.

At the start of chapters, are 'keywords' that operate as core concepts considered in the chapters. More significantly, they offer signposts to the major concerns addressed in the book.

Quotes from the text are sometimes highlighted, which suggest either an insight about animation itself or a particularly strident or apposite point of view.

At all points, the book seeks to raise questions and ideas, and to stimulate response and debate with the reader.

The **front and back sections** of the book are white and work as introductory, information and reference pages.

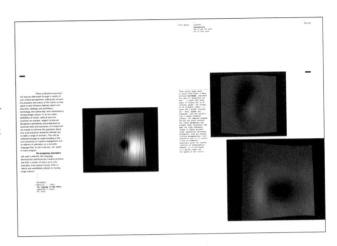

Front matter   Contents
                    Introduction
                    How to get the most
                    out of this book

010/011

HOW T
THE M
OF TH

The chapters start with a **chapter opener**. Each of the five chapters is given a specific colour, which runs through the section.

The structure of
levels of informa
text privileges th
words of the cor
provides the cen

accompanying ca
add additional in
further ideas.

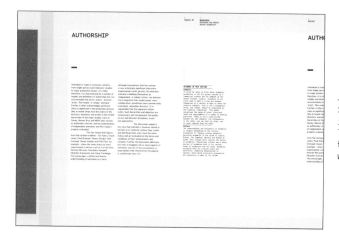

Sections within chapters are introduced with this spread. These spreads also contain the main keywords discussed within the section.

'keywords' that c
considered in the
they offer signpo
addressed in the

sometimes highli
either an insight a
or a particularly s
of view.

to raise questions
response and deb

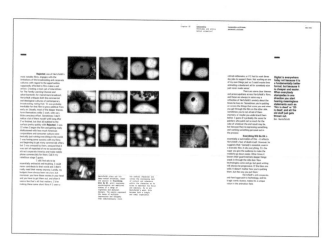

The text pages contain supporting captions and relevant pull quotes in order to demonstrate the main points within the body text.

TEACHING MOVING IMAGE CULTURE

—

PEDAGOGICAL IMPLICATIONS

—

01

THE
DISCIPLINARY
SHIFT

—

The changes in moving-image practices
provide a number of challenges in a range
of contexts. The artist or animator may
be liberated by new opportunities, but the
teacher, student and new practitioner must
re-engage with how their work is affected.
As well, the exhibitors, broadcasters and
corporate marketeers need to reassess
their needs. Disciplines are shifting;
orthodoxies are changing. It is clear that
digital technologies have prompted new
interventions and new processes, and
this in itself resets the agenda about how
the implications of these changes should
be addressed.

Chapter 01   The disciplinary shift
               Approaches and outlooks
               The bigger picture

014/015

**THE
DISC:
SHIF**

KEYWORDS IN THIS SECTION

Experimental

Within the field of animation, experimental
film has largely been cast as non-linear,
non-objective abstract work, engaging with
formalist issues concerning colour, shape
and line for its own sake. With the digital
shift, different perspectives on the
experimental have emerged as a result of
artists, animators, film-makers and creative
practitioners often using the same tools to
create work for different contexts and
purposes. All modes of expression - from
classical narrative to anti-narrative - have
been re-explored, freshened and re-subjected
to experimental approaches.

Dumbing down

Cultural debates in recent years have
been pre-occupied with the idea that Western
society is 'dumbing down'. This view is
largely characterised by accusations of
anti-intellectualism; over-investment in
celebrities and the banalities of 'reality
TV'; and a resistance to the notion that
traditional models of skill and knowledge
have been replaced by new capacities and
abilities in information and communications
technology (ICT). This discussion assumes
that society has changed and there has been
a de-historicisation and de-politicisation
of culture, which undermines effective
learning and progressive creative practice.

The changes in n
provide a number
of contexts. The
be liberated by n
teacher, student
re-engage with h
As well, the exhi
corporate market
their needs. Disc
orthodoxies are c
digital technolog
interventions and
this in itself rese
the implications o
be addressed.

NEW DIGITAL
ORTHODOXIES?

—

It is important to look at the indices and provocateurs of change in animation. It has historically been a field characterised by a variety of modes of expression, from the traditional cartoon through to the experimental film. Animation has always embraced new technologies and sought out ways in which new tools might facilitate new outcomes. It has always been, however, a form of expression, which has been easy to dismiss as 'the cartoon', or children's entertainment, or a mere vehicle of popular culture. On the other hand, it is the choice of the avant-garde, a modernist language, and the height of experimental cinematic achievement.

It is in the latter schism that animation has found its Achilles heel — it is at one and the same time an invisible art, or the art of the visible. It is a form destined to be defined ultimately not by formal conditions — frame-by-frame manipulation of materials in the creation of phases of representational motion — but by the artist, context and condition of expression. Arguably, nothing has changed. Animation has always re-imagined itself and is merely in a new phase at the heart of new digital orthodoxies. The difference lies in the fact that this is now acknowledged; and that artists and animators wish to re-engage with established parameters and definitions to re-establish or de-establish the term and the discipline of animation in alternative ways. This is ultimately the subject of this book. It also addresses the digital shift and the sense of change in current practice, and asks some key questions:

What drives/promotes/enhances this change?

—

In the educational field, do we talk about process for its own sake?

—

Should we focus on end users? How do they experience/assimilate/synthesise the information that is being expressed through these new modes of expression?
What exactly is the affect or effect of such work?

—

Are we really talking about something that is really new? The narrative may have evolved, but is what is being said progressive or original? Does it need to be? How should we determine meaning?

—

Will content ever shift away from the intrinsically human and maintain credibility?

PLEASE NØTICE
THAT I HAVE ØNLY
MENTIØNED ISSUES
ØF SEXUAL FREEDØM

THAT ARE
DEFINITELY
BARRIERS
TØ SEXUAL
EQUALITY IN
SØUTH KØREA.

IT WØULD BE IMPØSSIBLE,
IN THE CØNTEXT ØF THIS
ADDRESS, TØ DISCUSS
ALL THE FEMALE SEXUAL
INHIBITIØNS THAT ARE
MALE GENERATED

HERE IN THE
NØRTH, WHERE
LIFE CAN BE
DIFFICULT,

Chapter 01   The disciplinary shift   New digital orthodoxies?   016/017
                    Approaches and outlooks
                    The bigger picture

Young-Hae Chang Heavy Industries, featuring the work of Young-Hae Chang and Marc Voge, was one of the first key creative practices to explore the use of Flash animation in relation to text. Its piece, **Cunnilingus in North Korea**, deliberately plays with a contentious idea - the co-option of sex and sexuality for ideologically determined

outcomes - and a playful repertoire of expression within a specifically limited vocabulary. This is therefore 'cutting edge' in a way that students or practitioners can see as clever and provocative. However, it is different from mainstream work without being too alienating or abstract. It also has become an instantly recognisable signature style.

According to Chang and Voge: 'Our **Cunnilingus in North Korea** project came about when our dear leader saw the unique possibilities of the Internet for his message of peace and love.

We were, it appears, part of these "possibilities". We were looking for a cheap, easy way to do things. No expensive, heavy or space-consuming materials for us.

'As for process, well, we did what we always do, put text to music. As for technical and aesthetic choices, we chose one font (Monaco), two colors (black and white) and one technique (Flash). In our case, animation makes text move, movement being what makes art come alive. In art, those who know always talk about how this or that element of this or that composition "moves".

Well, it doesn't, actually. But now it does. And for some reason this makes people feel good. Though we did not start out with specifically political intentions, they did happen, it seems, but which, with the exception of the art issue, is for us beside the point. We're not out to convince people of anything. In fact, that's what makes what we do seem so beautiful to us.

'We didn't so much choose animation as we chose text (small file size) and music (irresistible) for the Web, the sum of which imposed animation (Flash) on us. We really don't follow the animation scene. On the other hand, we don't follow the art scene either. This, it seems to us, is what makes our work original: our ignorance of what's going on out there. Students: beware.'

WE NORTH KOREANS PITY YOU, BECAUSE MONEY AND THE BAUBLES IT BUYS HAVE BECOME MORE IMPORTANT TO YOU THAN SEXUAL PLEASURE.

WE SEE SEXUAL PLEASURE AS GETTING SOMETHING FOR NOTHING.

AND WE SEE PROLONGED SEXUAL PLEASURE AS GETTING A LOT AND GIVING A LOT, WITH ABSOLUTELY NO CAPITALISTIC BARTERING.

AND ENDEMIC TO CAPITALISM. SUFFICE TO SAY THAT

—

Arguably, under these conditions, new models of pedagogic strategy and delivery are desperately needed. There may be an immediate problem with the word 'pedagogy' though, as its premise seems to signal passivity. What can teachers, practitioners and artists do for students or prospective artists to make their experience a genuinely profitable one? One immediate response might be that educational contexts need to more properly recognise the many different professional and production outlooks. In some ways recognition exists, but it can easily lapse into an industry-fuelled obsession to produce the 'right' kind of student or practitioner with appropriate skill sets. This is normally an anomalous and homogenous view of the creative industries, un-interrogated by the particularities of skill shortages, contextual and regional needs, or the specificities of production. More importantly, and intrinsic to the perspectives addressed in this discussion, there is a lack of engagement with a 'bigger picture' in relation to the arts, society and commerce and the ways that the individual may be positioned in relation to the political, creative and economic demands of these contexts.

INDUSTRY REALITIES
—

As counterpoint to localised assumptions, it would be interesting to examine the realities of industry requirements a little more closely. There are certain pragmatic concerns that all students and prospective practitioners rightly have – usually, to get a job to pay off their debt – but what remains important is to enable students and creative workers to be able to fully understand the multifaceted nature of the industry and have more options

accordingly. It is likely that there needs to be pedagogical development or evolution to mirror changing professional and production modes, but it is clear that the philosophical foundation of educational or professional facilitation ought to establish creative principles that make skill transfer and cross-contextual play natural. It is therefore worth trying to define the differences between 'discipline' (in other words, ways of thinking qualitatively and quantitively; imperatives in work production; intention; consideration of audience paradigms; and the ability to think critically or expansively in and around the topic or task) and 'subject'.

Discipline is, for the most part, delivered within the context of a subject. At its heart, any imperative to support and promote creative work ought to define the tools that are vital to creative individuals. An understanding of context and need (potential or existing) enables students and practitioners to apply their disciplinary skills broadly, but it is important to instil a more fearless irreverence for accepted mores, in the desire to achieve progressive work and not simply 'tick box' outcomes. There are risks involved, as a 'world is your oyster' mentality might give rise to extensive production, but insufficient quality.

The explosion in self-publication, broadcast and authorship, and the development of abundant niche markets have prompted debates about dumbing down and the triumph of the 'new amateurism', effectively eradicating any clear distinctions about what constitutes good or bad work. It is clear, however, that this very occurrence has massive implications for the disciplinary shift and needs to be addressed as an 'anything goes' mentality that may

I thought differently from others and knew it was important to show that you could create a good story, show your creative skills and have a professional visual sense to show your technical quality.
Youngwoong Jang

Chapter 01   The disciplinary shift   New digital orthodoxies?   018/019
              Approaches and outlooks
              The bigger picture

drive this kind of abundance, serving to obscure important values and outlooks central to an understanding of the kind of creativity that might be progressive and enriching. This view may immediately prompt an anxiety that there is a desire in the outlook of this discussion to reimpose an elitist view of quality and a judgemental hierarchy reminiscent either of hard-line assessment processes within educational contexts or a reassertion of old-school arts culture values, but the proposition here is much simpler. It is crucial that more responsibility is taken for creative work. It is insufficient to merely be intuitively creative or driven by a creative fitness for purpose. Rather, it is necessary in such a climate to cultivate a conscious, focused and inventive clarity about creative endeavours.

        Consequently, a much greater degree of pressure resides with the artist, the pedagogue and the student to critically engage with and justify the nature, significance and purpose of what they do. Nothing can be learned if what is in place remains unexplained, un-interrogated or unquestioned. This discussion, therefore, seeks to track and show how such discourses might occur and how their outcomes are significant.

Youngwoong Jang, winner of the Academy for Motion Picture and Arts Sciences Gold Medal for best student film, **Mirage**, has some clear views about how a student might pursue a career in animation:'I had two goals to catch by making **Mirage**. One was having my first animation to establish my own voice through having a unique visual style. The other was to show my CG skills for seeking jobs. Some people said that it was very difficult to pursue two goals with one project, but I thought differently from others and knew it was important to show that you could create a good story, show your creative skills and have a professional visual sense to show your technical quality. I asked many classmates and teachers about how to get a job in the CG animation field - "be a generalist for smaller studios and be a specialist for bigger studios". It was the general answer I got. However, I believed achieving the best quality that I could attain within the time and resources available was appropriate to both. To improve the quality of my work, I showed it to teachers, classmates and as many informed people around me as I could. I listened carefully to their comments about my work and used this to analyse it and develop it further. I had been researching various areas of art, design, architecture and computer graphic animation. I trained myself in the areas of modelling, rigging, texturing, animation, lighting and compositing. I knew I wanted to work in various creative areas in the 3D animation field and I did not want to specialise. I made my demo reel to apply to CG commercial companies as a CG generalist in New York City. Actually, most of my reel was composed of **Mirage**. I tried to make a professional quality reel not like a typical student's output. Texturing and lighting were good areas that I could apply for in the major studios. I had an interview at Blue Sky Studios with the lighting team after they watched **Mirage** and I got a position as lighting technical director - the lighting supervisor told me he saw my lighting ability in my short film. Lighting is about the look of a film, and part of my visual sense, not just a technical skill. You have to have both aspects.'

Skill sets within the context of many educational training and production contexts inevitably aspire to transcend the practical and relate to research methodologies, critical thinking and contextual understanding. This is important as there is a clear attempt not to let the age-old theory/practice divide inform outlooks. The reality of many deliveries, though, is that theory and practice do remain not merely separate, but oppositional in the eyes of students or creative practitioners.

KNOWLEDGE AND SKILL SETS
—

Practical and technical knowledge is obviously important as it forms the skeleton of any creative process. However, overtly vocationally oriented outlooks can sometimes abandon critical ideas in favour of the cultivation of a particular type of operative – one who may not be capable of developing cogent ideas and only executing those of others. Some might argue that this is the dominant requirement of many working contexts, but it is surely not serving those contexts to good effect, nor reflecting well upon those who seek to educate with a more holistic perspective.

In the field of animation, this has been reflected by a range of people with high degrees of technical competency in the operations and applications of software, but no knowledge of traditional animation skills or, more importantly, no view of why they use the freedoms and limitations of their digital resources in the way they do. This is a consequence of not seeing that there is no theory without practice; no practice without theory; no progress without history, and the insistence that all outcomes must be goal-oriented.

It is important to constantly ask what educational contexts are producing. Does 'production' remain an appropriate term, for example? It is possible that the opportunity for creative experience may help to cultivate an attitude/aptitude that can transcend some of the more inhibiting aspects of traditional processes, especially if they maintain an unresolved tension between theory and practice. The ideal remains to produce imaginative, creative individuals who defy categorisation, and who in turn speak to the breakdown in disciplinary norms within the field of animation. Such a conceptual and disciplinary 'collapse' needs to be embraced by deliverers and institutions, who must maintain the principles that underpin a discipline, while ensuring that there is enough flexibility in order to constantly evolve a robust critical methodology.

All arts education should be about incitement, not about complicity, and this is something that the freedoms of expression in animation can readily accommodate. It is something that industry should recognise, but importantly, should not hope to measure, quantify or successfully co-opt. In many ways, industry should be co-opted more into educational contexts to encourage the richness of ideas, lateral and extraordinary thinking, breadth of vision and critical analysis as the key drivers in the evolution of the creative industries and the innovation economy.

There is no theory without practice; no practice without theory; no progress without history…
Paul Wells

Chapter 01   The disciplinary shift   New digital orthodoxies?   020/021
              Approaches and outlooks   Re-engaging definitions
              The bigger picture

RE-ENGAGING DEFINITIONS

—

In experiencing a disciplinary shift, animation needs then to once again reflect upon what it is, how it might be taught, and how it is received in institutions. The discipline and form of animation has been radically altered again, especially in terms of its context and in its changing roster of practitioners.

Other disciplines have in essence 'fed' animation, emancipating it from the two camps of commercial cartoon, with its character-based animation and experimental art practice. Regardless of the richness of these two strands of activity, animation and new moving image are manifested on every mobile device, LCD screen, feature film and website. It is apparent that a disciplinary shift, more readily embracing illustration, graphic design, architecture, product design, fashion idioms, interaction design and medical imaging has occurred and 're-imagined' the form.

With the democratisation of animation production, new potential philosophies of expression, easy vehicles of distribution and exhibition – MySpace, Facebook, YouTube, for example – there is some anxiety about the nature and definition of the form, and the ultimate requirements of the more established producers and providers as they reassess their next investment and market. This context provides the ultimate challenge for students and creative practitioners, but there is no reason why one should not service the other directly. This in itself should properly motivate the work and prompt the proper articulation of the factors that drive a piece of animation, moving image or motion graphics work. The will to communicate, the desire to act pragmatically and to problem-solve are ostensibly objective concerns pertinent to all artists, and are fundamentally at the heart of the re-imagining of animation in the contemporary era.

RE-EN DEFI

—

In experiencing
needs then to on
it is, how it migh
received in instit
form of animatic
again, especially
in its changing r

essence 'fed' ani
from the two ca
with its characte
experimental art
richness of these
animation and ne
manifested on ev
screen, feature f
apparent that a c
readily embracin
architecture, pro
interaction desig
occurred and 're-

of animation proc
philosophies of e
of distribution an
Facebook, YouTuk
some anxiety abo
of the form, and t
the more establis
as they reassess

APPROACHES
AND OUTLOOKS

—

So, what then are the new approaches and outlooks that characterise the re-imagined state of animation? Many, of course, sit within similar parameters to the past, but the conditions by which the work is done is now sometimes of a different order. Although animation has often been seen as merely children's entertainment, what does it now mean to engage the child in the multimedia, multi-distraction world of today? Indeed, how should the student respond to the social and cultural conditions that now prevail? Should the work undertaken operate as a premeditated calling card to appeal to some notion of the creative industries, or are freely expressed artworks enough?

This leads on to bigger concerns about the role and function of learning institutions, particularly concerned with how involved they should be with industrial contexts and how far a context in which the pure concerns of the animator or artist are dealt with and enabled.

Arguably there is more animation happening now than ever before, but so much of it is generated as a calling card, and consequently as a declaration and validation, that the creator of the piece can readily fit, not merely into an industry as it is currently configured, but into corporate culture in general. In such a context, should learning institutions accept a quasi-business identity wholesale and merely mediate between training and employment? Should they provide an alternative culture of innovation and experiment free from commercial constraints?

Many might conclude that one could easily facilitate the other, but this is surely about empowering individuals to develop new models of working that fail to recognise such a polarity and instead work in different ways. A final core aspect of the discussion is an exploration of how far this is possible and under what terms and conditions it might be achieved.

Chapter 01 — The disciplinary shift
Approaches and outlooks
The bigger picture

022/023

APPR
AND

—
—
—
—
—

KEYWORDS IN THIS SECTION

Research
Research is a term that is not sufficiently related to the outlooks and practice of creative artists, but it remains absolutely fundamental to the development of enriching and progressive work. Engagement with core questions and hypotheses; attention to processes and environments; and the creation of critically engaged material outcomes are all intrinsic to every artist's work, and these are part of the research necessary to inform provocative and developmental projects.

New traditionalism
In the contemporary era, the dominant 3D computer-generated aesthetic created by the artists at Pixar Animation Studios, Dreamworks Animation, Sony Pictures Imageworks and a host of other major Hollywood studios, has effectively replaced the 'classical' 2D animation styling of the Disney Studio. In essence, this aesthetic, as well as the narrative and thematic preoccupations of such films that feature it, constitutes a 'new traditionalism'. These works draw readily on the American cartoon tradition in general. This form of computer-modelled animation has, therefore, become the new classicism, which other works ape, react to, reject or critique, in the same ways as animation around the world for many years responded to the dominance of Disney as a style and a brand.

So, what then a
outlooks that c
state of animat
within similar p
conditions by w
sometimes of a
animation has c
children's enter
mean to engage
multi-distractio
how should the
and cultural cor
Should the wor
premeditated ca
notion of the cre
expressed artw

concerns about
learning institut
with how involv
industrial conte.
in which the pur
or artist are dea

RE-THINKING MOVING IMAGE PRACTICE – A COMPARATIVE MODEL

Innovation in any medium can be achieved through a number of means: the impact of new technologies; different trends in creative practice and critical analysis; shifts in cultural tastes and understanding; and, most significantly, fresh imaginative visions. Artists work in many different ways and, whether at the start of a career, or having endured the shifts and vicissitudes of arts culture over a long period of time, there is always the possibility of embracing a fresh opportunity or stimulus in the development of new work. This might arise out of a particular brief, an opportunity for collaboration, the formal development of personal preoccupations, or a re-engagement with the established codes, conventions, rules, expectations and achievements of a field.

Further, and this is particularly the case in animation, the capacity for the form to embrace and combine all arts disciplines and engage with cross-disciplinary, multidisciplinary or interdisciplinary interfaces with approaches and materials beyond the arts, means that innovation and progress is always possible, given the seemingly infinite possibilities available to the artist. With the dominant practice in animation taking place in the short form there is even greater variety, given that there are fewer generic formulas that the artist might feel compelled to follow. For the most part, then, the conscious choices made by the artist/animator define the outlook and originality of the piece and, ultimately, define the nature of animation itself.

In the digital era, animation has simultaneously re-engaged with its past and looked to the future. On the one hand, it has embraced its history and achievements more fervently and admiringly than ever in new books, documentaries, exhibitions, festivals and conferences. On the other hand, it has pronounced traditional forms; it is a thing of the past that has reinvented itself through new digital applications and processes.

DEVELOPMENTAL SHIFTS
—

Arguably, all the arts and most other disciplines have been affected by the impact of digital technologies, but it has always been the case that artworks seem to go through particular shifts in their development. In his book, **Hollywood Genres**, Thomas Schatz uses the work of Henri Focillon to describe this phenomenon:

—
'(Focillon)...observes that the continual reworking of a conventionalised form – whether it is in architectural style or a genre of painting – generates a growing awareness of the conventions themselves. Thus a form passes through an experimental stage, during which its conventions are isolated and established, a classic stage, in which the conventions reach their "equilibrium" and are mutually understood by artist and audience, an age of refinement during which certain formal and stylistic details embellish the form, and finally, a baroque (or "mannerist" or "self-

Winsor McCay's work, like that of many early cinema pioneers, was a mixture of trick effects and deliberate manipulations of images in what should be regarded as 'proto-animation'. This was part of animation's experimental phase.

United Productions of America (UPA) used modern art forms (such as in Mr Magoo) to challenge the dominant styling of The Walt Disney Studios and the cartoon comedy at Warner Bros. This was part of animation's classical period.

Chapter 01   The disciplinary shift
              Approaches and outlooks
              The bigger picture

              Re-thinking moving
              image practice –
              a comparative model

              024/025

reflexive") stage, when the form and its embellishments are accented to the point where they themselves become the "substance" or "content" of the work.' (1)
–

This trajectory can be readily traced in the history of animation, for example, where early pioneers in the United States, Japan, Russia and Argentina looked to establish the terms and conditions of the cartoon out of a combination of primitive cinema practices and indigenous arts in what was an essentially experimental phase. Although a number of animation practitioners were to develop work in the 1920s, it is traditionally and unsurprisingly acknowledged that it was The Walt Disney Studios that effectively created animation's 'classic' stage by establishing an animation industry, enhancing its technologies and applications, and developing its classical styling and aesthetic, which still survives – much imitated but much challenged, too – into the contemporary era.

The age of refinement in animation embraces a number of aspects: the redefinition of the Disney hyperrealist aesthetic in cartoons such as the work of Warner Bros Studio, United Productions of America and independent artists, as well as animation studios across the world including Halas & Batchelor in Britain, Soyuzmultfilm Studios in Russia, the Zagreb Studios in the former Yugoslavia and the Toei Studio Films in Japan; the recognition of experimental, non-linear, non-objective forms of animation, exemplified in the works of artists such as Norman McLaren and Oskar Fischinger; and the consolidation of other practices like 3D

stop-motion animation, cut-out and collage animation as developmental strategies in a continually emerging form. The baroque stage has essentially arrived with the digital era, from the earliest experiments with computer animation in the late 1960s and early 1970s, to the achievements of Industrial Light & Magic and later Pixar in the mid-1980s, through to the emergence of **Toy Story**. Finally, the availability of affordable digital equipment and software in the contemporary era has enabled a variety of artists, practitioners and animators to exhibit and distribute their works and moving images across a range of platforms.

There remains one key flaw in this trajectory. Animation has always been a profoundly self-reflexive medium, right from its emergence as a populist yet modernist art in all the contexts in which it found purchase and progress. Constantly aware of its own high artifice and illusionism, and the overt presence of an author always configured in the self-conscious nature of the image-making, animation has insisted upon its distinctiveness and potential difference, if not subversiveness as a form. As animator Jonathan Hodgson has noted:

> 'Whether you're an animation or a live-action director now, you're using the same equipment and tools – After Effects, Final Cut Pro, Photoshop and so on. But I do find my brain works in a different way when using all that equipment... because I have to think harder about the technical side all the time.' (2)

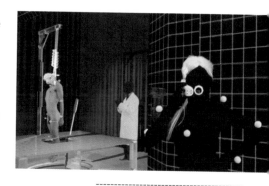

Contemporary practitioners, AL + AL, use all the digital tools at their disposal to create a new moving image palette, to re-imagine animation. This is part of the ongoing baroque trajectory in animated forms.

This is a pertinent point because it identifies the convergence of live action and animation, and also highlights the significance of the artistic choices that are being made in the use of technology and the model of technique. Ironically, the technology and the technique draw together the visual effects artist and the fine artist, as well as the traditional animator, the old media practitioner and the new media auteur. Inevitably, then, ideas about what animation is or might be have changed and it is only through exploring the nature of technology and technique that it is possible to identify, not merely the meaning and effect in any one work, but the particularity of its application in the definition of the form.

One example of the ways that this can be measured is in a project undertaken by the Victoria & Albert Museum, Onedotzero, the Institute of Contemporary Arts and Loughborough University. Very simply, a number of student practitioners took part in a project in which they were asked to create moving-image responses to a range of historical artefacts in the Victoria & Albert Museum.

Each student was encouraged to thoroughly research their chosen object in relation to its historical meaning and material culture. They developed a range of narratives in relation to an object, some choosing to reveal the object's meaning, others opting to imagine its place in a particular scenario. Simultaneously, the students themselves were defining their own aesthetic and technical practice, some choosing to call it animation, others film-making and some moving-image-making.

Fundamentally, the artist was naming the art and placing it within a particular kind of tradition, contributing perhaps to the baroque stage of animation history.

COMPARATIVE MODELS

—

The comparative examples here, **Incarnation** (2006) by Scott Allen, and **Object React: Vacuum Cleaner** (2006) by Naor Aloni, are both based on a response to the Dyson vacuum cleaner. The two bear comparison because Allen's film chooses a more symbolic and abstract response to the piece, and deploys animation in an inventive if quasi-traditional form. On the other hand, Aloni has used a more literal response to the artefact in a spirit of supporting a more realist narrative underpinned by visual effects.

Allen was inspired by the design of the Dyson vacuum cleaner and its innovation in domestic cleaning. He immediately recognised that there were a number of thematic issues that arose from choosing a state-of-the-art cleaning tool. He notes: 'I was not disappointed when I first saw this vacuum of all vacuums. The sexual connotations were just so unashamed I had to find out who, what, why and when. I began to look at the history of Japan and Japan today. I found out about Hiroshima and Nagasaki and the physiological effects this may have had on the country. I wondered, "Is this the reason the country has become materialistic to the point of obsession? Could materialism be a way of regaining control – a plastic plaster to cover one of humanity's greatest wounds?"'

Allen creates intimations of traditional Japanese pastoral values and pictorial iconography as an establishing premise of his film.

Allen uses the convention of 're-animation' drawn from the gothic narrative and 'mad science' to suggest the impact of modern technologies on organic life, here represented by the heart.

Chapter 01   The disciplinary shift
                Approaches and outlooks
                The bigger picture

                Re-thinking moving
                image practice -
                a comparative model

                026/027

Allen drew together particular themes prompted by the object, suggesting: 'My idea was to create a timeline from the moment of the nuclear bomb to the present day, then taking it forward to the warped future, where the human bond with technical advancements is concerned with absorbing our identity. Humans become nothing more than the possessions we judge ourselves by.' The themes that emerged were identified as a particular kind of efficiency represented in the functionalism of the vacuum: a sense of aversion to dirt and dust – our living 'debris'; a relationship to oppressive domestic identities, particularly for women; a kind of eroticism in the shape and form of the design; the connection with advanced technologies in Japan; the tentacle sex of Japanese anime and the phallic tubes associated with traditional hoovers; and the way in which identity can often be defined by technology – the age-old tension between humankind and machines. Ultimately, Allen felt: 'When you scratched the surface of the marketing, it was all about desire. From the product design to the diagrams on the box, the reference to the human body made me feel as if a housewife had morphed into her top-selling appliance. It was the best solution.'

These associations provided a ready platform for Allen's work and soon established a potential visualisation scenario in which a woman was redefined in the shape of a Dyson vacuum cleaner. It created a graphic metaphor that called up the associations suggested above, and made a particular comment about the specific kind of oppression endured by some women in Japan – locked into a traditional model of domestic subservience and service. Such a

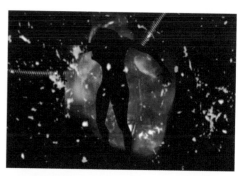

work serves to reconfigure not merely our view of an apparently ordinary, everyday domestic appliance, but reconfigures a whole range of issues about gender, technology and society.

Allen's work innovates in ways that cleverly use the tools available to him but, more importantly, in its use of ideologically charged and aestheticised imagery to offer up new meanings in contemporary visual culture. He challenges the assumptions embedded in material and social existence. In the same fashion that animation has always done, the compositional and juxtapositional elements of the piece offer up metaphysical and metaphorical meaning as a function of the image-making itself and not as a consequence of linear or literal storytelling. This is a very important aspect of the ways in which animation in all its configurations works. It is through the particular manipulations of the moving image, in whatever constructed form, that a high degree of meaning and effect are attained. More significantly, it demonstrates the authorial ownership of the image and its implications.

Naor Aloni felt that this degree of authorial ownership was a very important factor in determining the process: 'In retrospect, the difficulty with choosing an object derives simply from the potential available in any connection to an object to simply reinforce your general view as a visual artist. Some will argue that as a visual artist you can and should be able to put your signature on any project you're deciding to take on, and I agree, and should have probably chosen one with the furthest connection to me for the exercise and the

The transformation or incarnation of the woman begins, suggesting the tentacle sex of anime films and the reincarnation of the body in **Frankenstein**.

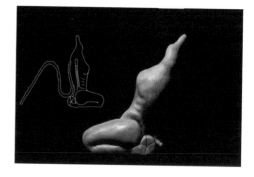

The transformation is complete as the Dyson domestic cleaner becomes the indistinguishable female body of the domestically oppressed Japanese woman.

challenge. I chose to react to the Dyson vacuum cleaner, though, because it already possessed some of the elements I wanted to see in my visual response. The object is powerful and beautifully designed, right down to the little details. The distinctive character combined with the functionality almost suggested a conflict, and after the early stage of research I thought that emphasising a clash of ideologies seemingly embodied in the design would be interesting.'

Research remains a fundamental component in the development of such work because it creates a potentially visual vocabulary from which to choose when finally creating the work. Allen's choices of place, event and outcome helped him to develop metaphoric as well as literal metamorphosis, using the freedoms of the vocabulary to extensive effect. Aloni, on the other hand, wanted a greater degree of control in the piece using the formalism of live action to represent a particular idea. The re-animation of the space as the instigator of the critical perspective underpins the piece. 'My idea was to create a tornado storm in a house. This was based on the principle of the cyclonic separation in the vacuum. Putting the movement in reverse helped me to emphasise the functionality of the object, while showing how a storm was putting things back in order.' This narrative conceit sought to show how the intrinsic chaos of existence has been measured, ordered and subject to repression; left to its own devices, the world is arbitrary and out of control, yet it is the cyclone here that re-imposes order.

Aloni insists that: 'My response was based on my intention to react to the object and not to present it. My aim throughout the first stage of research was to get to know the object, restricting myself from coming up with visual responses or ideas at that point. I did so by trying to gather any piece of related information I could get hold of and purely spending time with it, taking photos. For me, the risk of producing visual responses too early sometimes means falling in love with some ideas and not letting go. The second stage was to find any visual correlations within the information I had. At that point, linking the collection of visuals with the information on the object led me to some ideas.'

Here, there is one object, but two different kinds of re-imagining, playing out age-old tensions in cinema between the limits of live action and the freedoms of animation at a point in time when new technologies enable a complex mediation between the impossibly real and the possibly surreal.

The very tension at the heart of moving image practice, then, is also responsible for the variability of expression – at one and the same time form has become content and vice versa.

—
—
—

REFERENCES
1. Henri Focillon,
   'The Life Forms in Art'
   quoted in Schatz, T. (1993),
   Hollywood Genres,
   (New York: Random House)
   pp 37-38
2. Jonathan Hodgson quoted
   in Cook, B. & Thomas,
   G. (eds) (2006),
   **The Animate! Book:
   Re-thinking Animation,**
   (London: Lux / Arts Council)
   p 68

Chapter 01   The disciplinary shift   Re-thinking moving   028/029
               Approaches and outlooks   image practice -
               The bigger picture   a comparative model

Naor Aloni's work restores
social order through the
force of a cyclone. As the
world exhibits its chaotic
collapse, a cyclone revises
the sense of organisation,
repression and sobriety that
underpins a cultured dinner
event. This is the world
made clean and real, only
revealed by the disruption
of animation and the effects
of change.

RE-THINKING CGI AS A DOMINANT AESTHETIC

—

Since Pixar Animation Studio created the first fully computer-generated animated feature, **Toy Story**, in 1995, computer-generated 3D work has become the dominant form of the mainstream animated film, along the way replacing Disney's classical 2D styling as the core aesthetic of what Shiloh McLean calls 'new traditionalist' animation.[1]

McLean's term reflects the fact that Pixar, while innovating technically, has essentially embraced the well-established 'rites-of-passage/emotional journey' storytelling techniques of the Disney studio and the comedic verve of classic Warner Bros cartoons in a contemporary, but essentially traditional, model. Critical mass has now been reached in the computer-generated feature and the 'wow' factor of merely engaging with the fact that a film has been made using computer technologies has passed. This has led to a re-examination of the evolution of computer-generated works in a variety of national production contexts and, most particularly, an engagement with the ways in which animators and film-makers are using computer-generated imagery – a way that still reflects its presence as a mainstream aesthetic, which has been co-opted for personal statements.

Youngwoong Jang's Student Academy Gold Medal winning film **Mirage** (2006) was predicated on state-of-the-art, computer-generated animation and a personal meditation on life's intrinsic purpose: 'I have been trying to live a better and happier life by pursuing one goal and then another goal, constantly responding to my endless desire. When I came to New York,

I wanted to explore art, design and animation, and establish my own style by studying at MFA Computer Arts at the School of Visual Arts. **Mirage** is an autobiography based on life's uncertainty. In many religions, a question helps to provide a way to experience spiritual awakening. There is a question at the heart of Buddhist meditation: How can a pot, which is broken at the bottom, be filled with water? This question represents the problem of endless human desire. I thought that this idea could be developed into a story for my final year animation. I was also interested in the juncture between the organic and the mechanical, which I wanted to represent in my film. I wanted to draw something uncanny and create scenery that was dreamlike in **Mirage**, because I did not want to mimic the real world. I designed a robot character and added the fish character to give the robot a dilemma in which he might have to take another's life to survive and continue his own journey.'

Mirage boasts a high degree of technical skill in its execution of 3D computer animation, creating a futuristic boy-figure – part skeleton, part robot, part flesh and blood. He is obsessed with collecting water – seemingly his lifeblood – while, ironically, living under the sea. Jang cleverly illustrates how the single-mindedness of a person can blind them to other possibilities and alienate them from other points of connection or understanding. Although the boy reaches his goal of attaining more water for his water chest, it is only when he confronts a goldfish, equally in need

The biomechanical boy scales a reed in his undersea environment seeking out water - literally his lifeblood.

Yang successfully creates a new world, as suggested by the combination of organic and industrial forms and its place beneath the sea. It is a place that has a sense of both past and present, and a sense of strangeness, that contributes to the view of the loneliness and apparent alienation of the boy robot.

Chapter 01   The disciplinary shift   Re-thinking CGI as a dominant   030/031
              Approaches and outlooks   aesthetic
              The bigger picture

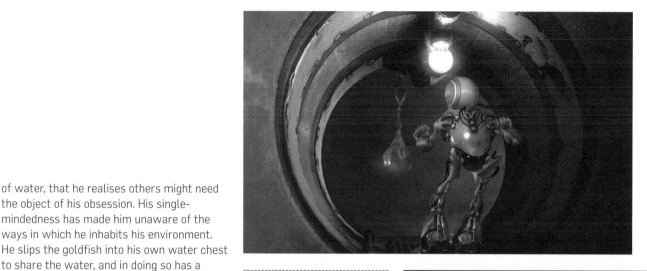

of water, that he realises others might need
the object of his obsession. His single-
mindedness has made him unaware of the
ways in which he inhabits his environment.
He slips the goldfish into his own water chest
to share the water, and in doing so has a
moment of revelation and enlightenment.
He can pursue his desires and needs, but in
a more inclusive and connected way.

  Jang suggests: 'The basic
concept of **Mirage** is that things can be
changed by shifting one's point of view.
Mirage has two levels. The first is about
learning to coexist and the second is about
the pursuit of happiness. Although the main
character seems to be on a never-ending
journey, I tried to express that happiness
may not be too far away. It is already in your
heart. When the robot climbs up the metal
object shaped like bamboo, I hoped the
audience would see a character struggling
to appease its endless desire. Like the robot,
I am living in New York City and looking at
many situations as a foreigner, and though
I have been living here for four years now,
I feel that I am still looking at the world
through etched glass.'

  The key to Jang's metaphor
is the creation of a particular world,
simultaneously related to some notion of
lived experience, but equally, a distantiated,
biomechanical and alternative existence,
which throws into relief its questions, and
possible meanings and effects.

—

—

—

REFERENCES
1. Shioh McLean, **The Art
   of Digital Storytelling,**
   Cambridge, Massachusetts
   and London: MIT Press, 2007

The boy confronts the
object of his desire - a
stem containing a droplet
of water. His search is
seemingly fulfilled, but
it is a moment that leads
to a more revelatory
understanding of
his existence.

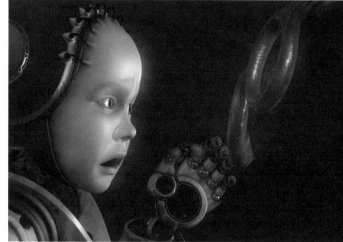

The boy robot is designed
in a way that reveals the
humanity of the child
principally through his
facial expression, often
starkly juxtaposed with his
mechanistic construction.
Here, there is a sense
of both horror and
fascination surrounding
his confrontation with
the bulbous stem and
the water within it.

The boy has a moment of
revelatory satisfaction as
he places the goldfish in his
water chest and essentially
reawakens his heart through
the realisation of sharing.
The metaphorical and
metaphysical meanings are
based on a simple idea
played out in an innovative
narrative world.

RE-THINKING
THE BROADCAST
CONTEXT

—

Although there remains a constant need for traditional models of animation for television that concentrate on character animation and simple, often humourous, narratives, it is also the case that visual and cultural literacy for children is changing, and there is a need to find different ways of communicating with them through inventive visual idioms and different approaches to the soundtrack.

Josh Selig, producer of **Wonder Pets!**, notes that: 'The series began as short films that we made for Nick Jr. These were called **Linny The Guinea Pig** and they featured Linny leaving her cage and going on adventures in outer space and under the ocean. Linny was animated to beautiful classical music by Tchaikovsky, but she didn't speak or sing, and she was all by herself. Based on the success of these shorts, we added Tuck and Ming-Ming and decided that these three classroom pets would use teamwork to save young animals in distress. I wanted to continue to use classical music, so we developed our current approach of having the characters both sing and speak their dialogue.' This use of music is challenging since the quasi-operatic form of expression is radically different from the idioms of the popular song used in most series. There is a distinct challenge to children to engage with unusual models of delivery potentially outside their cultures of experience.

In order to support the challenge of the soundtrack, Selig and his creative director, Jennifer Oxley, developed a fresh visual styling through a process called 'photo-puppetry'. Oxley notes that: 'The style combines the look of real photographs with the flexibility of animation. Using Adobe Photoshop, real photographs are used to create the backgrounds and characters. An average character will have three to four replacement head and body positions with a full set of mouths, blinks and eye positions. After all the pieces have been designed they are then prepped and animated using Adobe After Effects. The goal is to create animation that is both bouncy and fluid while staying true to the natural movements of real animals.'

In many senses, this approach, which echoes more craft-orientated forms like cut-out animation and collage, seeks to bridge the gap between the familiar animated series and the new image practices. Oxley adds: 'I tend to like animation where you can still feel the hand of the artist. Even though some of the computer animation being done today is absolutely phenomenal, there is still something magical about seeing a real brush stroke moving across the screen or slight fingerprints in an animated clay model.' Oxley's creative sensibility is influenced by a combination of her respect for Jim Henson's work on **Sesame Street**, the storytelling idioms of the Aardman studios, particularly in the recent **Creature Comforts** series, and her experience with animals: 'As a child I was in a programme called **Junior Rangers** and worked with an actual park ranger rescuing and taking care of sick and injured animals. It's funny that I'm now working on a television show about three classroom pets that save animals in distress.'

PHOTO-PUPPETRY
—

Selig and Oxley believe that it is especially important to empower pre-school children, so it was crucial to create a fresh approach to empathetic educational strategies. Selig stresses: 'It was important to me that **Wonder Pets!** not have any actual super powers. Linny, Tuck and Ming-Ming

I tend to like animation where you can still feel the hand of the artist.
Jennifer Oxley

The show's engagement with nature and animals is a key theme in the re-imagination of the animated form, explored at the conclusion of this discussion.

Chapter 01 The disciplinary shift Re-thinking the broadcast   032/033
         Approaches and outlooks context
         The bigger picture

are able to accomplish extraordinary things because they know how to work together and that's something that all young children can do. We chose a guinea pig, a duckling and a turtle for **Wonder Pets!** because we wanted variety, both in terms of what the characters looked like and what they could do. Their personalities were developed to reinforce their roles on the team: Linny is the leader, Tuck is the emotional heart of the group, and Ming-Ming is pure confidence. Every episode of **Wonder Pets!** has what we call a 'tieback'. This is a story beat that takes place in the classroom, which foreshadows a solution the pets will come up with later in the show. We also have recurring songs such as, 'The Phone Is Ringing!' and 'What's Gonna Work? Teamwork!'. I believe the mix of familiar songs and story elements with exciting new animals and locations has been a major factor in the success of **Wonder Pets!**'

    Little Airplane has re-imagined animation to enable children to re-engage with animals and not merely see them as cartoon characters, by prioritising a style that uses documentary actuality photo-animation, coupled with the melodramatic idioms of opera. Zinkia's work on **Pocoyo** returns to a simple aesthetic, prioritising the emotional and physical gestures of the characters, who for the most part play out their exchanges in empty spaces and environments. The use of global illumination and matte textures is much more reminiscent of clay than computer-generated imagery and contributes to the sense of tactility and physicality in the characters. Although the series draws on sources as varied as anime, it is the way in which the characters engage in a playful children's theatre that prompts a particularly immediate emotional and visual identification in the child viewer.

The playfulness of the narratives enable the characters to operate as perpetual performers. The use of music, dance and choreography successfully supports and conveys the idea of teamwork.

Photo-puppetry techniques revise the aesthetics of the children's series in **Wonder Pets!** and play an important part in presenting the animal to children as not merely animated characters.

The reference to super-hero stories in **Wonder Pets!** is radicalised by the ways in which collaboration, common sense and problem-solving acumen become the heroic everyday aspects of successful communication.

© & TM ZINKIA ENTERTAINMENT S.L., 2005

© & TM ZINKIA ENTERTAINMENT S.L., 2005

Zinkia's **Pocoyo** manages to refine the aesthetic of children's animated series further, privileging first and foremost the actions of the characters and the closeness of their relationships. The simple, clean design also enables the animation to embrace a range of engaging choreographic motion and events.

Chapter 01   The disciplinary shift
                    Approaches and outlooks
                    The bigger picture

                    Re-thinking the broadcast
                    context
                    Re-thinking educational
                    models

                                                                                      034/035

RE-THINKING EDUCATIONAL MODELS

The examples so far have both implicitly and explicitly engaged with ideas about how animation can educate as well as entertain or challenge. At the heart of this is a sense of rethinking what might be effective in relation to how animation, or moving-image practice, might be taught, and how animation might be used to teach related or other disciplines.

Finnish animator and guitarist, Mika Tyyskä, wished to combine these skills in an online delivery of guitar tuition, using the character of **Mr Fastfinger**: 'The whole thing started in 2000. I was studying at Lahti Institute of Design and I needed to come up with an idea for a multimedia workshop. I got the silly idea for an animated cartoon character teaching guitar playing. I made an interactive demo with a typical heavy metal guitarist character on the screen, playing simple riffs. I felt there was some potential with the overall idea.

'I returned to the concept in spring 2004 as I had decided to develop the concept as my thesis work for the school. I came up with the world of **Mr Fastfinger**, a character who is a sort of embodiment of all my guitar heroes. Steve Vai, Eddie Van Halen, Frank Zappa and Jimi Hendrix. For me this was a perfect project to work on as it included all the things that I've ever been interested in – from guitar playing to animation, from sound design to illustration, from interactivity to the transcription of music. I knew that there wasn't this type of content for guitarists on the Internet, so I saw an opportunity.'

DELIVERY AND DISTRIBUTION
—

Tyyskä represents a kind of practitioner who embraces multiple skills and disciplines as his core tools, and recognises that there are possibilities for new kinds of delivery and distribution: 'When I was 15 years old, I learned a lot of playing techniques by watching instructional videos of my guitar heroes. I often dreamt that when I was a famous guitar hero, I would be shooting my own instructional videos. Although that seemed like a joke at the time, making **Guitar Shred Show** felt like fulfilling this old dream in a cool way.'

The reception of the show reflects the diversity of the audience that can be reached even when this is seemingly a niche interest: 'The feedback I've received from all kind of visitors has been amazing. The project seems to appeal to many types of people from very different age groups. Many of the website visitors aren't guitar players, but they just love the experience. Guitar players, and especially young musicians, have found the website an inspiring source of learning, material and fun.'

Tyyskä recognised that animation could be deployed in a way that reconfigured the teaching video, replacing the teacher-guitarist with a fictional character who might have wider appeal. Tyyskä notes: 'As I was developing the overall concept for **Guitar Shred Show**, it was clear to me that I didn't want to create this for guitar players only. I didn't want to just do a guitar lesson, I wanted to combine guitar playing with action and

Tyyskä creates web pages that prompt investment in the act of learning the guitar, but which also entertain and inform in their own right.

fantasy. I believe that the younger generation is more aware that animation can be pretty much anything. We are not used to seeing animation used for everything yet, so combining animation bravely with new things can achieve interesting results and considerable attention.'

Inevitably, in attempting to re-imagine how animation could facilitate technical tuition, Tyyskä encountered problems, recognising that animating detailed figure positions for chords was difficult, but in essence, this wasn't at the heart of how he viewed education: 'I simply decided that my biggest mission with this project was to inspire everyone. For guitar players, it would provide musical inspiration, even if I wasn't able to explain everything in detail. For non-guitar playing visitors the inspiration can be found in the sensation of being able to jam like a guitar hero with the help of a computer keyboard.

'I had to resolve the biggest question, which was would anyone be interested in taking a guitar lesson from a cartoon character? To win the respect of guitar-playing users I did my best to make Mr Fastfinger as believable and as real a guitarist as possible. As a guitar player myself, I was able to create accurate finger animations. On typical cartoons, the characters just wave their hands on top of their instruments and it doesn't really look like they are actually playing. The animation can also be quite unmusical in rhythm and expression. This is something I really don't like in cartoons. With **Mr Fastfinger** choreography was also very important. It had to go tightly together with all of the riffs and licks. To get inspiration for the choreography, I watched a lot of music videos and live performances of Mr Fastfinger's role models.'

As well as contemporary guitar heroes, Tyyskä was influenced by the visual styling of Genndy Tartakovsky's **Samurai Jack**, a seminal cartoon series in its self-conscious use of a range of graphic design idioms. Crucially, Tyyskä feels that his inspiration doesn't really come from a 'top down' model where established artists and animators influence the next generation. He believes in a 'bottom up' peer model, which he can readily engage with through the Internet: 'One of my daily sources is blogs such as www.drawn.ca, which focuses on illustration, art, cartooning and drawing. I enjoy and get more inspiration from low-budget animations made by independent artists than high-end productions by big studios.' Tyyskä has developed his project further by taking it into a live performance context, noting that 'there are plenty of possibilities for mixing cartoon fantasy and real world.'

> **I enjoy and get more inspiration from low-budget animations made by independent artists than high-end productions by big studios.**
> Mika Tyyskä

Chapter 01   The disciplinary shift   Re-thinking educational   036/037
               Approaches and outlooks   models
               The bigger picture

Tyyskä recognises the
importance of enabling
guitarists to learn how
to play using computer
technologies that they may
use every day at school,
college and work.

Mr Fastfinger embodies
the shapes of contemporary
rock guitarists and
encourages empathy and
interest in guitarists, music
fans and the general public.
This is reinforced by the
creation of a fantasy world
related to similar mythic
and martial arts narratives,
which are often appealing to
a similar constituency of
largely male participants.

Mr Fastfinger and Tyyskä jam
together in a cartoon/real-
world combination.

THE BIGGER PICTURE

—

Tyyskä's work and outlook point the way to the increasing necessity to embrace cross-disciplines not merely in graphic and visual cultures, but in other areas of work and education and, crucially, into an engagement with the bigger picture.

There is often the tendency to create work based on personal preoccupations, or on formalist aesthetic enquiry, but it remains important to draw upon major issues and debates from the real world. Although a more contentious statement, it is arguably the case that particular academic disciplines and commercial contexts have significantly narrowed their fields of enquiry in order to preserve a set of presiding conditions about what they might represent, and which in turn preserve the core identities and ideas that sustain a conceptual, aesthetic or market-based status quo.

It is still often the case that a hierarchical position is adopted about the status of certain work and of specific arts practices. The high/low culture debate persists despite considerable work, which has clearly evidenced the value and pertinence of popular cultural forms in their own right. However, even within arts culture itself, the graphic arts — comics, graphic narrative, some aspects of graphic design, and certain 'cartoonal' forms — still have to argue for their status as 'art' as determined by established arts culture criteria. This discussion, overall, is engaging with this topic, but it is useful to address a particular example that reconciles the use of a graphic print form, which has been adapted as an animation, draws upon a personal story, and yet speaks to important historical and political issues.

Chapter 01   The disciplinary shift
               Approaches and outlooks
               The bigger picture

038/039

**THE E
PICT**

-
-
-
-
-

KEYWORDS IN THIS SECTION

Politicisation

One of the assumptions of this discussion
is the idea that contemporary culture is
less interested in history and politics,
privileging the 'here and now' and the
transient over what are arguably crucial
and critical lessons from the past. This
discussion suggests that the conscious
use of animation - and related art forms
- can recover history and politicise the
personal and professional context.

Modernism

While it has been argued that this is the
era of postmodernity, and the triumph of
postmodernism - effectively a decentred,
de-historicised, de-authored world subject
only to relativism, fragmentary ideologies
and reflexive ironies - it is argued here
that animation, in all its forms, succeeds
in maintaining a modernist agenda in
promoting new languages of politically
charged expression and artistic enterprise.

Tyyskä's work a
the increasing n
disciplines not n
cultures, but in
education, and c
with 'the bigger

to create work b
preoccupations,
enquiry, but it re
upon major issue
real world'. Alth
statement, it is a
particular acade
commercial cont
narrowed their f
preserve a set of
what they might
preserve the cor
sustain a concep
based status quo

VISUAL CULTURE:
GRAPHIC DESIGN,
GRAPHIC NARRATIVE,
MOTION GRAPHICS

—

In the contemporary environment, to have a particular stance about an issue is ironically sometimes perceived as limited and, in some senses, fixed. Alternatively, an insistence on authorship is seen as a resistance to postmodern attempts to resist such an identity. In this kind of culture, there can be a tendency to dilute a point of view, or submit to a high degree of relativity, which ultimately ceases to stand for anything. One of the consequences of this can either be an ignorance of alternative points of view or a prejudicial resistance to differing agendas, particularly beyond the exigencies of western cultures.

THE PERSONAL AS POLITICAL
—

Marjane Satrapi's **Persepolis** is a memoir about growing up in Iran. It offers an insight characterised by the politicisation of her gender and race identity, and is charged with ideological challenge by virtue, first, of its status as a graphic novel, and second, by its adaptation as an animated feature. Satrapi recalls the 1979 revolution in Iran, when the Shah was removed from power: 'This revolution was normal and it had to happen. Unfortunately, it happened in a country where people were very traditional, and other countries only saw the religious fanatics who made their response public.'

Satrapi's graphic novel shows a bigger picture of Iran beyond these received images and stereotypes. Of the evolution of her graphic novel she says: 'From the time I came to France in 1994, I was always telling stories about life in Iran to my friends. We'd see pieces about Iran on television, but they didn't represent my experience at all. I had to keep saying, "No, it's not like that there". I've been justifying why it isn't negative to be Iranian for almost 20 years.'

In many ways, this added a particular purpose to the development of Satrapi's work, not merely politicising the personal, but using an approach that sought the popular audience, while nevertheless radicalising the expectations of the graphic form she assumed it had. 'After I finished university, there were nine of us, all artists and friends, working in a studio together. That group finally said, "Do something with your stories". People always ask me, "Why didn't you write a book?" But that's what **Persepolis** is. To me, a book is pages related to something that has a cover. Graphic novels are not traditional literature, but that does not mean they are second rate. Images are a way of writing. When you have the talent to be able to write and to draw it seems a shame to choose one. I think it's better to do both.'

This is an interesting insight in itself, as it underlines how the traditional literary text is still valued above graphic forms, but, as Satrapi points out: 'We learn about the world through images all the time. In the cinema we do it, but to make a film you need sponsors and money and 10,000 people to work with you. With a graphic novel, all you need is yourself and your editor.' Learning about the world has been a key concern of this discussion so far, and Satrapi's observation points out the importance of embracing and advancing visual literacy. It is not enough to merely intuitively understand visual models – to be educated with them and through them requires that the teaching of visual literacy has increased attention and primacy in a range of curricula.

Chapter 01   The disciplinary shift   Visual culture: Graphic   040/041
               Approaches and outlooks   design, graphic narrative,
               The bigger picture   motion graphics

Marjane Satrapi's ground-
breaking narrative about her
upbringing in Iran has made
the successful transition
from graphic narrative to
animated feature. It speaks
to audiences about a
lifestyle, culture and
identity still largely
unknown or misrepresented
in the West.

From Satrapi's point of view, however, she stresses: 'You have to have a very visual vision of the world. You have to perceive life with images otherwise it doesn't work. Some artists are more into sound; they make music. The point is that you have to know what you want to say and find the best way of saying it. It's hard to say how **Persepolis** evolved once I started writing. I had to learn how to write it as a graphic novel by doing.'

By evolving the work in this way though, the artistic imperatives in the novel were always allied to the desire to say something specific and challenging: 'I'm a pacifist. I believe there are ways to solve the world's problems. Instead of putting all this money to create arms, I think countries should invest in scholarships for kids to study abroad. Perhaps they could become good and knowledgeable professors in their own countries. You need time for that kind of change though. I have been brought up open-minded. If I didn't know any people from other countries, I'd think everyone was evil, based on news stories. But I know a lot of people and know that there is no such thing as stark good and evil. Isn't it possible there is the same amount of evil everywhere?'

Satrapi's position here rightly shows how the power of the global media has shaped the ways in which people think of other cultures and philosophies, largely to the detriment of other nations characterised by religious or political difference. Satrapi's open-mindedness and creative sensibility is deployed, therefore, to use art to challenge the conflict imperatives of the news media, to encourage a greater understanding of other cultures, and to promote more constructive initiatives in education through shared knowledge. She adds: 'If people are given the chance to experience life in more than one country, they will hate a little less. It's not a miracle potion, but little by little you can solve problems in the basement of a country, not on the surface. That is why I wanted people in other countries to read **Persepolis**, to see that I grew up just like other children.'

NEW AUDIENCES

Like Tyyskä, Satrapi is finding an audience beyond the anticipated constituency. 'It's so rewarding to see people at my book signings who never read graphic novels. They say that when they read mine they became more interested. If it opens these people's eyes not to believe what they hear, I feel successful.' Crucially, this also bridges a culturally invested generational gap.

This becomes a crucial aspect of Satrapi's outlook with the graphic novel's adaptation into an animated film. The work is reaching more audiences while not sacrificing the original novel's graphic look or its ideological content. Satrapi champions the role of the artist as an open-minded, visually literate, yet philosophically engaged person, and it is this model of creative endeavour that this discussion readily encourages.

That is why I wanted people in other countries to read Persepolis, to see that I grew up just like other children.
Marjane Satrapi

Chapter 01   — The disciplinary shift
               Approaches and outlooks
               The bigger picture

— Visual culture: Graphic
design, graphic narrative,
motion graphics
Art or ambience?

042/043

ART OR AMBIENCE?

—

Tomato, a major international graphic design company, has employed a version of 'ambient animation', which is correspondent to the 'nothing matters' ambiguity of some modernist practices. Often, such work enables companies to work successfully in a corporate marketplace by making this ambiguity – saying nothing in a manner that postures as good and particularly clever design – supplant the message. This is not about being tame with what one says, but it is strategically about saying nothing at all.
This can operate as a pertinent model – a postmodern impersonation of art – in itself. The nature of the intelligence and value of such work, of course, becomes questionable. Is such art, design and animation contributing to the dumbing down of the culture, but suggesting that vacuity in the imagery is as valuable as authorially determined views? Given the insatiably hungry range of cross-platform media eager to embrace content, sometimes in whatever form, art or animation that does not pose a question of itself, or indeed attempt to answer one, may be simply encouraging opting out, not thinking and not having a critically engaged sensibility. This essentially defrauds the visual.

Animating banality or
re-engaging with a modernist
idiom of 'nothingness',
commercial sequences can
often be groundbreaking and
reflect some of the less
engaged aspects of
contemporary culture.

ART C

—

Tomato, a major
company, has en
animation', which
'nothing matters
modernist pract
enables compani
a corporate mark
ambiguity – sayi
postures as good
design – supplan
about being tame
is strategically a

pertinent model
impersonation of
of the intelligenc
of course, becom
art, design and a
dumbing down of
that vacuity in th
authorially detern
insatiably hungry
media eager to en
in whatever form
not pose a questi
attempt to answe
encouraging optir
not having a critic
This essentially d

NG

S

THE POLITICS OF PRACTICE

—

—

02

TH
OF

0

AUTHORSHIP

—

Animation is made in numerous contexts, from single-person, back-bedroom 'studios' to major production houses. As a field, therefore, it is characterised by a number of models and definitions of authorship that can accommodate the terms 'auteur', 'director', 'artist', 'film-maker', or simply, 'animator'. Further, it often acknowledges particular roles as significant in the production process. Only in recent times have the claims of the directors, animators and artists in the Fordist hierarchies of the major studios, such as Disney, Warner Bros and MGM, been viewed as authorially relevant, and the achievements of independent animators and film-makers properly evaluated.

This has meant that figures from the cartoon tradition – Tex Avery, Chuck Jones, Paul Driessen, Osamu Tezuka, Paul Grimault, Dusan Vukotic and Pritt Parn, for example – share the same status as more experimental creatives such as Yuri Norstein, Norman McLaren, Alexandre Alexeieff, Kihachiro Kawamoto and Oskar Fischinger. This encourages a unified and diverse understanding of animation as a form, although assumptions that the cartoon is less artistically significant than more experimental works persists. By extension, animators labelling themselves as 'independent', or indeed 'artists', are deemed more important than studio-based, more collaborative, sometimes more commercially orientated, 'animation directors'. It is regrettable that this apparent schism exists. Such hierarchies and dialectics are unnecessary and misrepresent the quality across and between disciplines, styles and approaches.

This discussion supports the view that animators, however named or termed, or in whatever context they create and distribute their work, have the same status and are evaluated on the terms and conditions of their achievements and contexts. Further, the discussion addresses how this re-imagines one or more aspects of animation, and any of the assumptions or expectations that characterise the popular or uninformed view of it.

AUTH

—
—
—
—
—

KEYWORDS IN THIS SECTION

Commerce

It would be naïve to think about animation production in all its guises outside of a commercial context and the demands of the market economy. Clearly, animators of all kinds need to make a living and prepare themselves in a variety of ways to enter the creative industry. This is not a homogenous thing, and indeed, should be understood as the creative 'industries'. This model recognises the range of roles, functions, needs and requirements of a number of working practices. There is not a rigid divide between art and commerce; one infrequently is the other; one can fund the other; one is never removed from the other.

Culture

The understanding and evaluation of animation is largely determined by the culture evaluating it. Popular culture generally perceives animation in the idiom of classic Disney, The Simpsons, Wallace and Gromit or anime. Arts culture still resists the notion of animation. Educational culture has a mixed opinion of animation both in its various forms of production and its study. Animation struggles with its cultural place and definition, remaining marginalised or ignored, while being ironically progressive and subversive in many of its idioms.

Animation is mad
from single-pers
to major product
therefore, it is ch
models and defin
accommodate th
'artist', 'film-mak
Further, it often a
roles as significa
Only in recent tim
directors, animat
hierarchies of the
Disney, Warner B
as authorially rel
of independent ar
properly evaluate

from the cartoon
Jones, Paul Dries
Grimault, Dusan V
example – share t
experimental crea
Norman McLaren,
Kihachiro Kawam
This encourages a
understanding of a

ART AND COMMERCE

—

In the context of what might be said to constitute great art (or indeed, just art), the great irony is that despite animation's ability to transcend political, geographical and generational barriers in conveying and delivering a message, it is still often viewed as insubstantial and lightweight. Animation is still considered innocuous and juvenile, despite its proven usefulness as a primary propaganda tool in Maoist China, for example, or indeed its proven efficacy as a ubiquitous repressive and manipulative political tool in Western corporate media.

Equally, as a generally replicable and distributable mass medium or form, animation has largely been deemed undesirable by an art world immured in a very different commercial model. This seeming innocuousness is very useful, and the acceptance of it as a distinctive characteristic of the form by art culture, or immersion of it within the art world and its commercial markets, is distinctly undesirable. This is especially so if animation is to be further groomed and maintained as a highly effective and (very interestingly) trustworthy medium for the delivery of corporate directives.

THE CHILDREN'S AUDIENCE
—

A high majority of mass-media animation is aimed at children and generally manifests itself in one of two distribution channels – broadcast media or gaming. Animation within gaming has been following familiar formats, but it has lately emerged as a distinct and very interesting new strand: behavioural training.

Nintendo's **Animal Crossing** is a game aimed at the very young and employs animation to foster specific social skills and life lessons in children. **Animal Crossing** introduces capitalist values (working for a living, mortgages or consumerism) and a never-ending, but increasingly hard-to-achieve aspirational level of luxury and opulence. Through it, one is schooled in social benevolence (for profit) and envy. There is no discernible end to the game, or indeed any real objective. One simply climbs the property ladder and experiences, accepts and actively perpetuates the obsolescence that broadly drives consumerism.

Chapter 02   Authorship   Art and commerce   048/049
                 Attitudes and ethics
                 Artist animation?

Similarly, **Nintendogs** is also rich in life lessons. One is taught the virtues of patience and obedience, and is schooled in aspiration and competition. In both games, however, there is an unseen but omnipresent lesson in brand allegiance, a subliminal engendering of affection for a faceless Japanese corporation. Interestingly, through the adoption of the 'cute', both games are particularly successful in disguising the less-than-cute origins of the technology that they use.

Likewise, children's broadcasting proffers a seamless diet of life lessons and codes of morality endemic to Western orthodoxies that is designed specifically to provide respite from, and create a disingenuous context for, high-impact political propaganda – television advertising. Where once advertising was peripheral to children's television, the medium is now entirely dependent for its existence upon revenue streams from global industry. The majority of children's animation exists as a 'wholesome' vehicle to dispense advertising messages – as well as to lend a perceived innocence, frivolity and innocuousness. Television advertising takes this a step further by adopting the language of animation to dress its directives in primary colours and unlikely physics.

It is therefore not surprising that the art world is less inclined to take animation seriously when it has come to largely embody a corporate language that, unlike contemporary art, so obviously wears its industrial heart on its sleeve. Unlike the washing powder claims of efficacy fed to mothers between **Peppa Pig** and **LazyTown**, it is evidently somewhat hard to shift the traces of the original, corporate, industrial military agendas that conceived much of the technology used in contemporary mainstream animation, if the primary conflict-based concerns of gaming are anything to go by. In the light of CGI, the persistent juvenilisation of animation to lend innocence and stealth to adult agendas demands understanding and attention.

In the light of CGI, the persistent juvenilisation of animation to lend innocence and stealth to adult agendas demands understanding and attention.
Johnny Hardstaff

COMMERCE AS ART

—

Beyond children's television programming, the heaviest use of animation is without doubt to be found in corporate advertising and promotion. Through recent technological developments, the tools and processes of animation have been largely adopted and defined by graphic designers, as if by default. The designer's transition from 'commercial artist' to 'director' has not been without implications or repercussions. It has had a significant impact upon the direction and the underpinning ethos of graphic design and what were once modernist roots steeped in social value and social change. From television advertising through to online promotions and onwards to architectural visions of future corporate ventures, it is the graphic designers who are often driving animation, despite the heaviest use of animation now being largely servile in its purpose.

THE NEW GRAPHIC DESIGN
—

Designer/directors are not, broadly speaking, imparting messages of social value. They are less activists, and more like industrial messengers. They may package the message, but they do not design its content or its meaning. Graphic design has become the natural home of digital animation, and in turn, graphic design has therefore become an industrially directed service industry. It is important to consider why this has happened. Designers have perpetually chased authentic and refined aesthetics, born from a former

frustration (pre-CGI) of not being able to hone imagery of the highest 'artistic' quality. This former desire, once sated, has borne a practice. Arguably, in an age defined by the post-war engineering of BMW et al, that highest aesthetic is often best embodied in the physical output of mass-production. CGI technology offers this aesthetic mimicry to those who wield it. Electronic media offers the opportunity to play at an industrially determined aesthetic level that has in some way – largely through the efficacy of advertising – come to represent excellence.

From the mid-1990s until very recently, animation appeared to be on the cusp of a revolution at the hands of a new group of users who, through ignorance and lack of formal animation training, and unencumbered with any great legacy of process, were suddenly and widely working in moving graphic image. Animation became more prevalent, and this 'digital revolution' in moving image became most notably embodied in a raft of media organisations, such as Resfest, Onedotzero and the large number of 'animators' that they championed. However, the graphic designers were widely uncomfortable with the term 'animation'. They felt that the term did not represent what they were doing, and that it failed to recognise that they were doing something different to, and significantly more progressive than, the worlds of **Peppa Pig** and **Toy Story**.

Of all the objects we had to choose from in the Object React project, I found the statue, Kharamukha Samvara, the most visually stimulating – it looks like a freeze frame from a soap opera cliffhanger.
Selina Steward

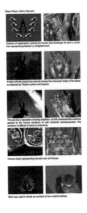

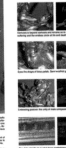

Preparatory materials for Selina Steward's Kharamukha Samvara project.

Chapter 02   Authorship   Commerce as art   050/051
               Attitudes and ethics
               Artist animation?

In adopting the John-Whitney-Sr-coined 'motion graphics' (his electronic film-making company 'Motion Graphics' was formed in 1960) some 35 years later, designers had taken a once-experimental definition and applied it in a fundamentally flawed manner, failing to recognise both the sheer breadth of existent media and the potential within not only animation, but also graphic design itself. Most tellingly, in dropping the word 'design' from the definition, 'motion graphics' also dropped the process of design from its animation activities and instead largely focused on an over-reliance upon corporate software to deliver message-free, 'content-lite' material. In so doing, corporate policy invaded the vernacular and the aesthetic of what should have been, and what was once, counter-culture. The messages of Honda were now brought to you courtesy of Autodesk, and the messages of despair or change were barely brought to you at all, and if they were, they were shaped by one of only three major software developers.

In the advertising agency JWT's (J Walter Thompson) in-house magazine **JWT Now**, Aart Jan van Triest, Vice President of Marketing Foods, Unilever Asia/China, explains how they prepare for the unexpected, and what role innovation plays in this: 'We prepare for the unexpected by staying connected to what I call the "dark side" of society – by understanding people who live out-of-the-ordinary lives, who already live parts of life that will become mainstream in the future.' Indeed, and whilst flippantly expressed in the language of **Star Wars**, within this reference we see the common commercial approach to subversion and dissent, which is namely to undermine through appropriation and consumption. The same magazine profiles JWT's new state-of-the-art post-production division – www.thenursery.tv – a unit designed to generate animated shorts for 'the kind of young male viewer who is spending more time watching shorts on YouTube and Google Video than sitting through TV ads.'

It goes on: 'Within JWTwo, the ad industry's largest and most technologically advanced in-house production unit, is a New York-based romper room for art school graduates – hand-drawing and digital animators, line artists and illustrators. Together they create the kind of raw, digital animation that will take hold on social media sites and allow JWTwo to learn more about how media is shared online.' JWTwo Director of Emerging Media, David Rosenberg, notes that through creating these 'anarchic' and 'irreverent' animations, the important thing it does for JWT is build relationships with video-swapping sites: 'To be able to pick up the phone, speak to someone at Google or YouTube and get preferential treatment is going to benefit our clients when it comes time to apply lessons learned to their business.'

Though these forms of creation and distribution may appeal to some people wishing to work in the creative industries, there is considerable concern about the content generated. As notions of subversion and counter-culture persist, it seems that the revolution will not only be televised, it will be streamed, screened and podcast, but it will also be entirely without

Selina Steward immediately recognised in the Kharamukha Samvara a tension between its dramatic possibilities, its aesthetics and its symbolic intention

Interestingly, it was the aesthetic aspects that were initially more important as there was a direct correspondence between the sense of geometric plasticity and artifice in the brass statuette and the specific kinds of representational forms available in computer animation.

substantive opposition, or recognition of alternative perspectives. To achieve within this context takes a significant re-imagining of possibilities and potential.

The democratisation of software has been principally held up as a significant contributor to the development of motion graphics and the liberation of creative talent, but democratisation is somewhat of a misnomer in this instance. Whilst CGI technology has been made more widely available, it is characterised by the presence and influence of a limited number of large software developers. Indeed, the level of corporate control over moving graphic aesthetics is not something that other genres of animation have either been restrained by or so obviously visually infected with.

This is important in the ways in which other approaches might be imagined and executed. Evidently, this may be one of the first revolutions that has occurred from the top down. Arguably, this controlled and manufactured revolution, with its origins in corporate governance, finds its exponents unwittingly substituting the possible visual languages of a counter-culture for that of an ongoing succession of software releases. How should artists and animators respond to this seeming contradiction?

Artists have to find a way of working that is either complicit with the tools and outlooks that they are afforded, or find some way of subverting these models, either through a different kind of manipulative technique, or more likely through the ways in which established image cultures might be challenged or reconfigured.

Selina Steward, in part, addresses this in her work on the Kharamukha Samvara, a Tibetan deity, often represented through brass statuettes, one of which she based her animation upon: 'A statue of a rare Tibetan Buddhist deity from the highest level of tantric teaching, the ass-headed Samvara, embracing of the "Wheel of Supreme Bliss", represents the transcendence that results from tantric meditation. He is in sexual union with his consort Vajravarahi, symbolising enlightenment through the blissful union of compassion and wisdom. Under one foot he crushes a female figure, Kalarati, "Night of Time", who represents nirvana – liberation from suffering. Under the other foot he crushes the male figure of Bhairava the Terrifier, who represents Samsara – the cycle of life and death.'

This correspondence served the dual purpose of creating a contemporary visual styling to the piece, while equally speaking to the Dalai Lama's stated intention that in the face of Chinese occupation following the 1949 military coup, artefacts should embody Buddhist teachings and reach an extended audience through their aesthetic appeal. Ultimately, there is some irony in this as the Samvara is a sacred, contemplative object; its shift both in context, and ultimately in its representational status as an animated object, inevitably changes the meaning as well as the effect of the object as a symbol.

Steward suggests: 'The Samvara is a deity for Buddhist meditation; the embodiment of a philosophy and a role model for the person meditating; an idealised form of the Buddha he aspires to become. The privilege of viewing the object is usually reserved for practitioners who have received the appropriate initiations. The object depicts fierce rites of destruction and sexual yoga and was kept restricted so that the uninitiated could not misinterpret the dramatic symbolism.'

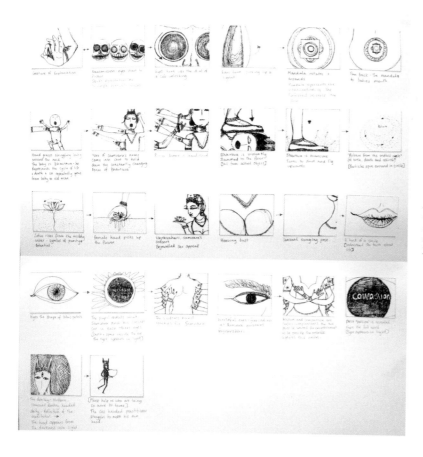

Steward continued her research on the piece in order to facilitate not merely the dramatisation of the symbolic ideas in her animation, but to engage with Buddhist teachings in the service of narrative: 'I intended to show the object being "called into action" and attempted to divulge some of its secret wisdom. I wanted to play on the misconceptions that prevented the object from being revealed; what looks like gratuitous violence is actually the fight to end suffering, and what looks like seduction is really about obtaining enlightenment more quickly. The tradition in Tibetan art is to represent multiple layers of information in one piece, and it can be a visual overload. I wanted to simplify the imagery.' In literally calling the object into action, Steward deploys animation to interrogate the image systems at the heart of Buddhist thought. Revealing some aspects of the metaphors at play in the statuette also prompts other layers of interpretation, particularly for Western audiences.

Object React. Selina Steward. 1 of 2

The bronze hands of the statue of Samvara. The hands are posed in the gesture of explanation. Echoing this gesture helps to form a mystical connection with the deity.

The hands come to life. The wheel symbolises the Buddhist law. It spins and opens like a safe containing precious information.

The skulls that are draped around the deities body, begin to transmit information.

Once they are activated we start to decode and explore the symbolic elements of the statue.

The practitioner enters the deity's realm confused, disoriented and wearing the head of an ass.

The ass head engages with the skulls transmitting mystical information.

A mandala opens around the practitioner signalling the beginning of a journey.

A baby is seen being threatened by the arms of Samvara. There is a disturbingly menacing atmosphere.

There is shock as Samvara attacks the seemingly innocent baby.

We witness a fierce rite of destruction.

The baby begins to grow.

He grows from baby to boy to man to old man and then dies. The sound of his constant suffering can be heard.

Our actions (karma), determine the level of the souls rebirth after death. As the man dies he is reborn at a different level.

The man keeps being reborn. The perpetual nature of this cycle means that there is no end to the transmigration of the soul.

This is revealed when the wrathful face of Bhairava the terrifier is exposed to be the true identity of the baby. Bhairava is the god who represents the perpetual cycle of rebirth.

Samvara overcomes Bhairava,

and crushes him under foot.

Now Samvara is released from the perpetual cycle of suffering and rebirth.

The final piece is insightful and reveals a philosophical and spiritual outlook, while equally foregrounding the graphic design and art-led computer-generated idioms of the contemporary era. The work has an elevated mystical sensibility and a genuine correspondence to progressive animated film. There is some irony in the observation of two Tibetan lamas from the Jamgon Kongtrul Labrang, who, although not well-versed in art film or the possibilities of animation, after seeing the piece, noted that 'everything comes from and dissolves into emptiness'.

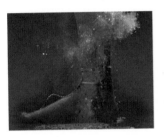
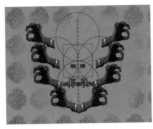
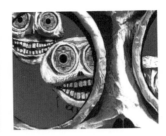
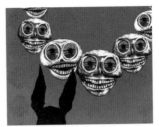
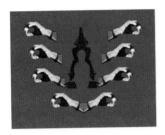
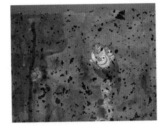
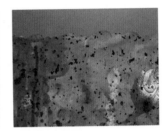
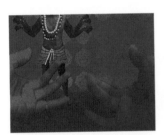
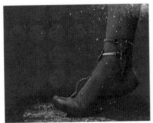
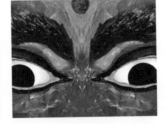
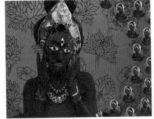
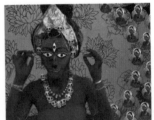
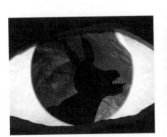
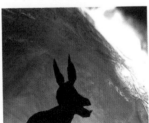
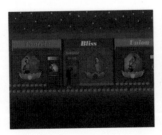
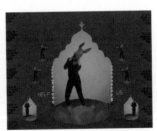

Chapter 02   —   —
           Authorship   Commerce as art   054/055
           Attitudes and ethics
           Artist animation?

Selina Steward's engagement
with her object prompted
a range of narrative
options, which she suggests
through her dramatic and
aesthetic choices.

The rise of dominant corporate aesthetics corresponds with the emergence of postmodernity and the conditions of postmodernism. Anathema to graphic design's modernist roots, the validity of saying literally anything that postmodernism has seemingly permitted and validated, has essentially devalued everything. Suddenly, it has become far easier to say nothing and even this has been embraced by postmodern aesthetics. A model of conservatism has ensued. A culture of saying very little has evolved, if not actively and purposefully, and where once within graphic design, for example, success might have been expected (the optimism of Ken Garland might be a good place to start) it is now often consigned to a mere gesture, which sometimes will not only suffice, but be treated as positively radical. Within the field of animation, this is made yet more complex by the variety of work, which on the one hand receives the validation of arts culture, while on the other, is dismissed as mere 'cartoon', even in its newly configured computer-aided, facilitated or modelled forms.

Further, the animation industry, at one and the same time a production context in its own right and a utilitarian application and language of communication permeating virtually all other creative and corporate production, apparently determines how animation should be understood. This problem often underpins how educational contexts determine their ethos and delivery, which is predicated inevitably on measuring future success by 'meeting industries' needs' – not redefining or refining industrial needs, nor even challenging them, but instead meeting them – surely an impossibility in the light of the diversity of the creative industries?

CHALLENGING EDUCATORS

This discussion suggests that it is crucial to challenge and question the complicit stance that educational institutions sometimes take in this respect. Formerly, it would not have been unlikely for once radicalised arts-based institutions to be the sole place looked to for innovation and ingenuity. It is important that arts education resists surrender and in some ways challenges its financial sponsors and clients with less reactionary agendas and perspectives.

Arguably, the commercial industrial arena is not a forum where new, dangerous or innovative things happen. Nor indeed do socially benevolent things happen within industry, unless there is a significant profit to be made at the expense of other things. If the new, the dangerous and the innovative cannot happen in educational contexts then they cannot happen at all. The great irony is, of course, that this is happening at a time when individuals do have unprecedented access to remarkable means of creation and global, uncensored mass-media distribution. The opportunity for a political voice to be heard is now as never before. The author has been facilitated, but the impetus needs to be taken up, explored and meaningfully engaged with.

Chapter 02   Authorship   Commerce as art   056/057
               Attitudes and ethics
               Artist animation?

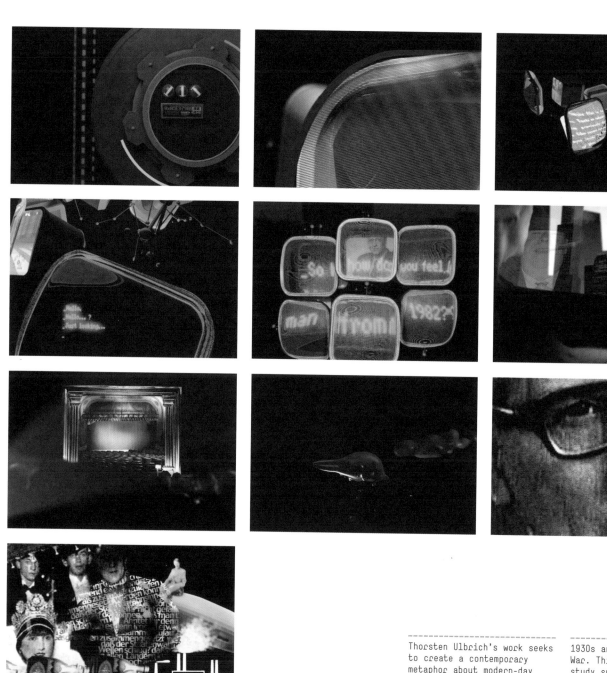

Thorsten Ulbrich's work seeks to create a contemporary metaphor about modern-day Germany that reflects some aspects of its deeply problematic, political, ideological and humanitarian issues during the period of National Socialism in the 1930s and the Second World War. This intends to be a study suggesting that contemporary Germany is imbued with the effects of the past, even as it tries to forget, move on and find salvation in its modern culture.

Thorsten Ulbrich has worked professionally as a designer, developed works in educational contexts and undertaken personal projects, being preoccupied by the questions of how best to create work and the social agenda of the work itself.

He recalls: 'I had worked for some years as a designer and seen different approaches to problems in art and graphic design. As a student, I was very concerned about the narrow-minded, market-driven concepts expressed at my college. Depending on the clients, briefs or intentions of the artist, there can be unhelpful market-made constraints, or simply the will of the client can often dictate the outcome of a work. But I consider art and design as a vehicle to provide a creative solution to a given problem. There are more creative disciplines allied to art or design, from writing to acting to animating, and so on. For me, creativity represents a Weltanschauung – an attitude towards the world. There is room for personal, emotional, daring, original and uncommon approaches in design and it can make sense to favour individuality against conformity and mass compatibility.'

There is some irony in the fact that Ulbrich's film, **Deutschland, Deutschland über Alles**, looks at this very tension, but from the highly charged and complex perspective of the nature of resistance to oppressive and conformist regimes and, most particularly, the Nazi regime in Germany before and throughout the Second World War, a subject close to his own background and interest: 'As soon as I saw the book, **Deutschland, Deutschland über Alles** by Kurt Tucholsky, I knew it was

something I could reflect upon and say the most about. The book was written in pre-Nazi Germany (1929) and was meant as a warning against the upcoming regime and its politics. As a German born in 1974, I was educated about the Third Reich; nevertheless I still have many unanswered questions about the time. My parents were born in 1939 and my grandparents were in their thirties during the Second World War, so I am fortunate to have always learned about the period from personal accounts from them. I never really thought about it like that until recently, but I would have liked to talk with my grandparents about certain issues, such as the question of their possible "guilt", for example. But they are both dead now and there will never be a chance again.'

He adds: 'I know from my grandfather that it was a difficult time for him, in the beginning of the Nazi regime. He fought the Nazis as a member of the Reichsbanner, a social democratic alliance to protect the Republic. Later he had to join the German army, fighting for the Nazi ideology simply to protect his wife and two sons from repression and punishment for not obeying the orders. Now that I have reached a certain age, I am interested more and more in how the average German felt during the time, people like my grandparents or my parents, not the familiar faces portrayed in the media. The book deals a lot with doing the right thing at a difficult time and standing up for your values and opinions. It was written before the Nazis came to power and Tucholsky is widely acknowledged for his early prophetic warnings. His daring texts, together with the montages of John Heartfield, went against

For me, creativity represents a Weltanschauung – an attitude towards the world. There is room for personal, emotional, daring, original and uncommon approaches in design and it can make sense to favour individuality against conformity and mass compatibility.
Thorsten Ulbrich

Chapter 02   Authorship   Commerce as art   058/059
                  Attitudes and ethics
                  Artist animation?

the grain and totally polarised many readers, yet still managed to be constructive and positive in their suggestions.'

Interestingly, these stands against prevailing and oppressive regimes have characterised a great deal of animation both during the Second World War and the oppressive intervention of the Soviet Union in countries of the Eastern bloc. Animators almost uniformly made abstract or metaphorical works, which in their lack of an explicit position and their condition as animation – understood as an innocent medium even then – subverted the system and avoided suppression. Although artists such as Jan Svankmajer in Czechoslovakia found their work banned, the work of artists in Zagreb, for example, worked without censure.[1]

Ulbrich wanted to relate Tucholsky's ideas to the present day and create a narrative that reflected enduring issues: 'Upon reading the book, I felt like it hadn't lost any of its power. Everything is still pertinent to the politics, economy and society of today. Looking at neo-liberal politics and trade policies, the educational system, the decline of moral values, religious extremism and fundamentalism, hegemony and demagogy, I often feel that these are dangerous developments, leading to a possible catastrophe. I think it is important and interesting to deal with the question of how to make up one's own mind in a system of blind faith and mainstream acceptance. Significant differences between today's society and that of the 1920s and 1930s notwithstanding, I think that we could have

learned from past experience how to protect ourselves from mass demagogy, whatever it may try to influence us with.'

Ulbrich's approach, however, sought to use animation to partly re-animate history and to draw attention to the manipulation of the media in the facilitation of the mass consumption of ideological principles. This enabled him to work with contemporary graphic design and animation idioms to explore how similar kinds of inculcation occur in relation to late capitalist societies. Using antiquated televisions and outmoded graphics as an image of 'modernity gone wrong', Ulbrich points out the complicity of arts cultures and mass media in reinforcing and 'en-culturing' a particular status quo, privileging those in power. Terry Gilliam once remarked that although the future was supposed to look like the modernist city of **Things to Come**, it actually looks like the cluttered, often unkempt and disorganised, uniformly overstocked shopping mall.[2] Ulbrich's abstraction of the key issues is unashamedly committed to making the viewer think about the work and not become complicit in an explicit or too easily accessible narrative. This, of course, is creative risk. Ulbrich adds that: 'The downside of this approach, though, is that it demands a lot of attention of the audience in order to be readable and understandable, which is something that we have lost as a consequence of the mass media and the constraints of our fast-paced world.'

Most of the animators and artists participating in this discussion see their work in a spirit that foregrounds art as an important presence in its own right, offering insight and revelation about material culture and alternative perspectives about the human condition. These are clearly social values and not those predicated on the needs of industry. While such practitioners value the importance of animation in these respects – and this is the case across the history of animation – animation has often been marginalised from key academic debates and contexts. Film studies and film theory within the Academy has often absented animation from critical dialogues, which is at the very least curious given the range that animation has and the uses to which it is put, and in an era where film studies is in danger of losing its object to the post-photographic, digital world.

ANIMATION: A DISPUTED DISCIPLINE
—

When animation is addressed, it is often looked at in the context of cinema. This then immediately limits the way it might be understood, how it might extend its potential, and the applications it might embrace or inform. The other aspect to this is that, given the diversity of animation as a form, it can find itself delivered in a variety of environments within educational institutions, from computer science to media studies to art and design. While on the one hand this recognises the place of animation in a range of significant contexts and disciplines, it also dilutes its presence and focus as a discipline in its own right. While this has to be accepted and developed as a way of extending the field of animation studies, it significantly

problematises the way it might be taught and made influential. One only has to watch one cinematic gaming interlude to recognise the deeply undesirable effects of not enabling animation to develop a unique and strong body of critical theory, given that the manipulated moving image – animation in all its applications – is our most culturally ubiquitous visual manifestation. Ironically, animation is arguably the victim of an enduring hierarchy in the traditional arts. There are often misleading assumptions about its purpose and effect; even more so as animation is the core visual language in an age when messages can be conveyed in the subliminal blink of an eye, while the relevance of cinema is increasingly challenged.

Animation is repeatedly underestimated and this discussion seeks to stress the importance of understanding animation within contemporary society. If animation has been co-opted for the purposes of merely delivering corporate agendas or the mere aesthetics of difference, then it remains crucial to remember what animation might deliver as a language of free expression and possible subversion.

—

—

—

REFERENCES
1. Wells, P. (1998)
   Understanding Animation,
   London and New York:
   Routledge
2. Interview with Paul Wells,
   December 1994

Chapter 02　　Authorship
　　　　　　　 Attitudes and ethics
　　　　　　　 Artist animation?

Commerce as art
Corporate critique,
personal visions

060/061

CORPORATE CRITIQUE, PERSONAL VISIONS

In the light of the rise of corporate idioms and the expectations implicitly at the heart of this, the personal responses and outlooks of individual artists become increasingly significant and valuable. While this is not necessarily political or aesthetic resistance as such, it is, nevertheless, a necessary response to dominant models and the intrinsic conservatism of supposedly progressive imagery. Don Hertzfeldt, in films such as **Rejected** and **Everything Will Be OK**, represents an excellent example of a positive engagement with this climate of creativity.

TRADITIONAL HARDWARE
—

Hertzfeldt re-imagines animation in the contemporary era by going back to basics. He notes: 'I shoot everything on a beautiful old animation camera that was probably built in the late 1940s. Now I guess I'm one of the last people on earth shooting animation traditionally on 35mm film like this, which is a scary thought because I simply could not have made my last few movies without this camera. Many of the visuals, not just all the experimental shots, would have been impossible to capture digitally and extremely difficult, if not impossible, to simulate in a computer.

'Digital tools do certain things very well and film cameras do other certain things very well. One will never be "better" than the other, they're just different, but there's a herd mentality in the industry. Digital is everywhere today not because it is a fundamentally better format, but because it is cheaper and easier. In many ways it is more practical and that's to be expected, there's nothing wrong with that, but when everybody stampedes in one direction you start hearing meaningless statements such as "film is dead" or "2D is dead", and all the old stuff just gets thrown out. We should be expanding our toolbox when we add new technologies to it, not subtracting at the same time. So instead of having 100 years' worth of amazing film-making toys to play with, artists today are working with software and cameras that are rarely more than a few years old and that bothers me because it means all these artists have little choice but to essentially work from the same palette – and in animation especially, you begin to notice how everyone's movies sort of start to look and feel the same.'

Hertzfeldt is a self-trained animator who initially worked on VHS. While at film school he was drawn to animation as it was a cheaper form to work in: 'I think I've always approached animation from a strange angle, a bit like a regular film-maker, who just happens to animate. Editing, writing, sound, direction, those are the things that usually come first in my head. Animation is often just the busy work I need to get through to connect the dots and tell the story.

'In theory, animation is the purest way to make a movie. You can physically craft every frame of the picture by hand and that is a really powerful thing. You're not forced to make compromises – you're not limited by the weather, an actor's performance, or running out of time on set. Animators are free from all those restraints of 'reality', yet historically, animation has been the most misunderstood of all film and media. Early on it was branded a children's format and most animated films today are only made to sell toys. Others are little more than technology test reels. Ironically, places where you'll find animators are places where they are asked to achieve photorealism, rather than get away from it! It is a bit rarer now to actually find animators who are really free to explore.'

Don Hertzfeldt's breakthrough success, **Rejected**, makes a stinging comment on the banality and facile nature of American commercial culture and its implied moral and ideological agendas.

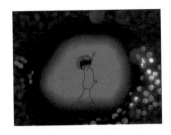

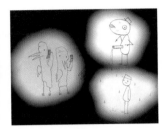

Rejected, one of Hertzfeldt's most notable films, engages with the limitations of the broadcasting and corporate cultures with regard to the opportunities supposedly afforded to film-makers and artists. Creating a mock set of interstitials for The Family Learning Channel and advertisements for mainstream broadcast, Hertzfeldt critiques both the commercial and ideological cultures of contemporary broadcasting, noting that: 'It was probably inevitable for that film to grow political from early on. Usually, most of the deeper themes form themselves while I work, with very little conscious effort. Sometimes I don't notice a lot of them myself until long after I've finished, but that all bubbled to the surface pretty quickly with **Rejected**. I was 22 when I began the film and getting really disillusioned with how much American corporations and consumer culture were basically just ruining everything in the world. I was having some success with my films and beginning to get many commercial offers, but I was annoyed by them, annoyed that it was sort of expected of me to successfully attract corporate America and make mobile phone commercials for them. Call it my rebellious stage I guess.

'I still find ads to be essentially antisocial and insulting. I could never contribute to that world and I didn't really need their money anyway. Luckily, my budgets have always been very low, but moreover, you have these movies in your head and you have to get them out, and often it seems like that's all that matters. I'd be making these same short films if I were a

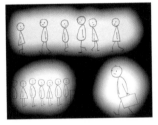

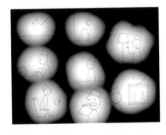

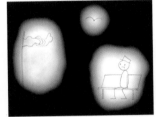

Hertzfeldt plays out his deep-rooted anxieties, fears and passion in **Everything Will Be OK**, which expresses psychological and emotional states in a range of vignettes and abstract designs. The panels represent the sense of multiple impressions and thoughts that simultaneously visit his central character and convey the increasing lack of control and coherence within the character as he tries to maintain his focus and identity. As in all Hertzfeldt's work, this becomes both a tragic and comic experience.

Chapter 02   Authorship
             Attitudes and ethics
             Artist animation?

Corporate critique,
personal visions

062/063

retired millionaire, or if I had to work three day jobs to support them. Not working on one of my own things just so I could waste time animating a deodorant ad for somebody else just never made sense.'

There are some clear themes and preoccupations across Hertzfeldt's films, and these are always in some way a reflection of Hertzfeldt's anxiety about the times he lives in: 'Sometimes you're putting on screen the things that scare you and when you get through the film on the other side, sometimes you're not afraid of them anymore, or maybe you understand them better. I guess it's probably the same for painters who paint not so much for the sake of whatever the end result may be, but because they're expressing something, and working something personal out in the process.'

Everything Will Be OK is essentially a summation of this – it reflects Hertzfeldt's fear of death itself. However, he suggests that: 'Comedy's essential, even in a dramatic film, it oils everything. It's the sugar you give the audience to make the medicine go down easier. Other times it lowers their guard and lets deeper things sneak in through the side door. New technologies come and go, but good writing will always be progressive. If the ideas are solid, it doesn't matter how you're putting them, but the way you put them.'

Hertzfeldt's anti-corporate, anti-herd approach to technology, and his tragic-comic stance, makes his a unique vision in the animation field.

Digital is everywhere today not because it is a fundamentally better format, but because it is cheaper and easier. When everybody stampedes in one direction you start hearing meaningless statements such as 'film is dead' or '2D is dead', and all the old stuff just gets thrown out.
Don Hertzfeldt

COLLABORATION
AND PURPOSE

—

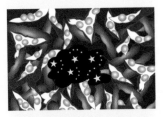

Myriam Thyes, in her online and public screen collaborative project **Flag Metamorphoses**, worked with a number of other artists and animators to play out ideological and political preoccupations as they were embodied in the symbols and aesthetic resonance of national flags. Thyes explains: 'For the last 15 years my themes have dealt with symbols, myths and visual signs from architecture, politics, films or religions. My works are explorations of their meanings – a questioning, a reassessment, a "destabilisation" and a creation of new associations. In order to undermine entrenched representations, I work directly with them to develop them further, transform them and then juxtapose them against new representations. I use animation, abstraction, collage and found footage (video stills) to present critical views of the current political, (psycho-) social, cultural and religious systems. I reconsider abstraction and graphical aesthetics as a means of critique in our over-saturated media culture, proposing that simplicity and imagination can still move us.'

Thyes's work is a very particular response to what she describes a very human 'double wish' to have both an individual identity and yet belong to a bigger group, often represented through nations, which are themselves 'imagined communities'. On her choice of flags as iconic stimuli, Thyes recognises that their symbolism often endures beyond the actual conditions a nation lives through, sometimes remaining largely aspirational: 'Flags have become very significant again during the last few years – in sports, politics and fundamentalist propaganda. In 1996 and 1997, I worked with flags as installations in public areas: I created and painted new designs and symbols on flags and hung them beside and between official flags. In the last three years, I started working again with themes I had used before in painting, drawing and photo assemblies, but this time with animation.'

Working in such a direct and politicised way, Thyes saw the opportunity to embrace both a democratic approach to the creation of work responsive to a core theme while engaging with other artists, but also in relation to its dissemination to a global audience on the World Wide Web: 'Thanks to the Internet, I got the idea and possibility to open the flag animation project to other artists, and so it started growing. **Flag Metamorphoses** lays stress on the relations between nations as changing ones: only in the permanent recreation of values, symbols and ways of life, in mixing with others and differing from others, that identities, cultures and societies stay alive. I gather as many individual and international points of view about flags as possible. I approach artists, designers and whoever is interested in contributing to **Flag Metamorphoses**, through mailing lists, websites, personal invitations, lectures, workshops, presentations of the project in exhibitions and festivals, and every possible way.'

Inevitably, this level of engagement prompts differing approaches and levels of interrogation. The political level looks at relationships between neighbouring countries, colonial ties and cultural imperialism. On the other hand, the artistic level examines the collapse and revision of largely geometric forms into more amorphous, organic and fluid configurations.

Since 1995, China has lost more than six million hectares of arable land to cities, factories, roads and deserts. At the same time, soya bean imports from Brazil to China have increased 10,000 per cent. The pulses are now by far the most important item on the bilateral balance sheet. Myriam Thyes addresses these issues symbolically in her film.

Chapter 02   Authorship   Collaboration and purpose   064/065
                      Attitudes and ethics
                      Artist animation?

Thyes herself has created a number of flag transitions – one dealing with the Spanish invasion of Mexico; another the centrality of Calcutta to the religious, cultural and economic tensions between India and Bangladesh; further, the colonial exploitation of the Congo by Belgium and its Western affiliates. Much of the **Flag Metamorphoses** deals with conflicts as this was the original context in which the flag found its purpose. It is Thyes's view that 'peace can only be achieved and maintained if people can create, celebrate and adapt their own symbols of identity, and respect the symbols of others.'

IRONY AND EXPLOITATION
—

British digital artist, Rona Innes has created a flag metamorphosis addressing the relationship between Malawi and Mozambique, where internal strife – flooding, drought, endemic poverty and overwhelming debt – has contributed to the ease with which colonial exploitation of rich mineral resources has taken place.

Innes uses the common colours and forms in the flags of the two nations to play with the irony that the countries' pride in their landscape and resources – including uranium, gemstones and gold – has been significantly undermined by warfare, extreme climates and the actions of the Portuguese in Mozambique, and the British in Malawi. In both, black represents the people of the African continent, and green symbolises the land and the enduring evidence of the maintenance of nationhood.

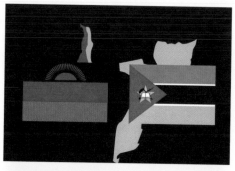

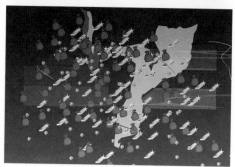

Rona Innes's reflection on the neighbouring countries of Malawi and Mozambique focuses on the colonisation and exploitation by the British and Portuguese. The subsequent inability to sustain economic growth, or be free of debt, and the attentions of indifferent global brokers are also issues that are addressed.

In both flags, red is concerned with the struggles for liberation from colonial oppressors and is associated with the blood of the martyrs in the cause of freedom. The difference in the intrinsic outlook of the countries is best expressed through the symbols on the flags, though: Malawi's rising sun suggests the dawn of hope and freedom for the whole of Africa, while Mozambique's rifle, hoe and open book offer a mixed message of a belief in literacy, democracy and working the land, facilitated by militarist defensiveness and authority. The Mozambique flag is the only flag to feature a rifle.

German-based American artist, Barry Roshto, has created a piece called **Red and Yellow**, which deals with the evolution of the Vietnamese flag and notes: 'One of the most formidable events of my childhood and teenage years in southern USA was a conflict which I had absolutely nothing to do with. It happened in a place that I have never visited, involving a nation of people with which I have had very little contact. But the war in Vietnam, with all of its traumatic effect on US society, is only a brief episode in the ancient and ongoing struggle of the Vietnamese people. This struggle is evident in the evolution of the Vietnamese flag. Although it has taken on diverse form, borrowed symbolic content from colonial powers, and remains a subject of heated debate even today, there is a central thematic thread: red blood and yellow skin.'

Roshto sophisticatedly uses the changing flags that have emerged out of Vietnam's complicity with, and resistance to, colonising influences as the subject and object of his piece. It begins with the original Chinese flag of the late emperors; the flags and related symbols of the French colonial oppressors; Vietnam's own internal divisions and preferred identities related to the rise of the Viet Minh; and the inevitable shadow of the United States, along with the impact of the Vietnam War.

Myriam Thyes recognised that the key concept of changing cultures was readily revealed through the use of animation's core language of metamorphosis, and in the way animation could reveal and yet challenge the dense meanings embedded in national image systems: 'Animation is a wonderful and perfect way to express transformations and recreations. The abstract and graphical language of Flash fits with flags and other symbols. When working with Flash, I can look at the result immediately and make changes quickly – this resembles drawing, painting or other direct techniques. Some people may think animation doesn't support art because they only know the commercial use of it, but even in the commercial sector, Japanese anime feature films contain a lot of artistic imagination.'

Conceptually, Thyes felt that the best results might be achieved if the metamorphoses themselves took place within a single frame: 'What I have in mind is generally one changing image, not a film with scenes and cuts. I prefer morphs and transformations, a scene that develops by metamorphoses and replacements of objects and shapes, in order to avoid the change of the complete image at once.

In Barry Roshto's film, the pre-1876 Chinese flag with its emperor dragon conveys the emergent impact of the People's Republic and the strength of South Vietnam, which is symbolised in the red spot.

The fleur-de-lys and Marianne are symbols for the French Republic and the struggle of the ordinary citizen. These intrinsic French symbols impacted on and influenced Vietnamese peasant lives.

Buddhist ideologies begin to conflict with French cultural identity. It is epitomised in the juxtaposition of a Buddhist prayer pagoda and a winged dagger from a French paratrooper's badge.

Chapter 02   Authorship   Collaboration and purpose   066/067
               Attitudes and ethics
               Artist animation?

FORMALIST APPROACHES
—

This use of the formalist limits of the frame,
while addressing the conditions of transition
and meaning within it, reflects Thyes's
background and identity as a visual artist.
The particular influence of Russian
constructivism and the work of the Bauhaus
movement are reflected in her collage
technique and political satire.

Her cinematic influences
are also pertinent: 'I like Pedro Almodóvar
for his photography, his image composition
and his use of colours, and, of course, for
his deep humour. I also like the experimental
and rhythmical films of Maya Deren, and the
mixture between video and animation.
I admire films such as **Antz** or **Shrek** as
intelligent entertainment, but visually it is
not what I'm looking for when it comes to
new experiences in animation. I think there
is much more to explore and there are many
undiscovered possibilities in animation.'

St Joseph's Cathedral in
Hanoi, styled after Notre
Dame in Paris.

French colonial power is
challenged and undermined
by Vietnamese resistance,
epitomised here in the myriad
of tunnels created by the
Vietnamese in order to
transport resources and
facilitate guerrilla warfare.
This approach undermined both
French and American military
and political power.

An image symbolising the
vying tensions between
residue French colonialism,
the rise of Vietnamese
communism and the
schisms of political
tension and conflict.

Roshto composed an American
flag using the icons of the
fallen soldier and prisoner
of war (helmet, rifle and a
bowed head) to allude to the
56,000 killed or missing in
action. The starless
(stateless) blue section
symbolises the four million
lost vietnamese.

ATTITUDES
AND ETHICS

—

Animation can often be treated as the 'innocent child' of contemporary media, perhaps due to the seemingly juvenile uses it is largely put to (albeit in the service of distinctly adult agendas). This association is still regularly bound up with the perception of the cartoon – animated features mainly made to appease younger audiences – and many stop-motion series made for television.

In the digital era, and in an age in which animation is understood as a mature arts medium, it can be deemed a stance. A temporal record of a psychological state. An emotional memory. Effectively, an invocation of mind. Either radicalised or complicit, it is the animation and realisation of our dreams. It is the animus. It is breathing life. It is the internalised animation of our thoughts made external. However, our animated political thoughts are rarely ever made external. The generation of patently political animation, represented in the resistance of animators living under repressive regimes or through periods of conflict, seems a thing of the past, despite the need for more alternative and oppositional perspectives. Culturally, there is a sense of 'de-historicisation' in the fragmentary conditions of postmodernity.

Humankind needs the cultural and historical background of existence, recording, examining, processing, preserving and re-examining in order to resist the loss of identity. With the loss of identity, there is nothing to calibrate ourselves against. Without the capacity for assessment, then there can be no resistance. Arguably, humankind in the West is witnessing the steady erosion of the capacity for dissent, and there is a need to realign more animated art and film with politics, ideology and material culture.

ATTI
ETHI

—

—
—
—
—
—

KEYWORDS IN THIS SECTION

Radical
Art has always sought to reflect, idealise,
interrogate and reveal culture; in turn
it has comforted, disturbed, elevated
and challenged in equal measure. In an
increasingly fragmented world, arts
cultures speak to niche audiences, and
experimentation in the form of a recognised
avant-garde has been made relative and
specific. To achieve a radical perspective
in these conditions is increasingly
difficult, but can be achieved through
a re-engagement with ideology, ethics
and aesthetics.

Re-contextual documentary
Animation has always embraced documentary
forms. The apparent artifice and illusionism
of the animated form is reconciled with the
non-fictional parameters of the documentary
form by prioritising the subjective
intervention in representing social and
cultural issues. These 'naïve' authorial
voices re-contextualise documentary codes
and conventions. They prioritise personal
perspectives; reposition received knowledge
in the form of 'grand narratives', and
respect different forms of knowledge and
different versions of the truth.

Animation can o
'innocent child'
perhaps due to t
it is largely put t
distinctly adult a
still regularly bo
the cartoon – an
to appease child
stop-motion ser

age in which ani
mature arts mec
stance. A tempo
state. An emotio
an invocation of
or complicit, it is
realisation of our
It is breathing lif
animation of our
However, our ani
rarely ever made
patently political

02

Essentially, there is a contradiction – in what should be a period of divergence and opportunity, there is instead a cultural narrowing where there is less statement-led vision and more literal work. Within this context there is a redefinition of the word 'radical'. It has lost much of its sense of challenge and has come to mean simply anything that has a diluted, predictable and vague political slant; anything more confrontational has become somehow unapproachably extremist. A prime example of this would be the work of Banksy. Politically vague and naïve, its diluted non-messages have found a highly lucrative commercial niche on the commercial periphery of the contemporary art scene, falling somewhere between the White Cube and poster shops. There is clear recognition that new contexts and modes of invention are required. In the field of animation this is taking place in what might be termed 're-contextual documentary'.

DOCUMENTARY STYLES
—

There is an established tradition of imitative documentary, echoing established documentary stylings in the travelogue and cinéma vérité, for example, and an increasing amount of work in subjective documentary, featuring singular voices as the embodiment of a 'naïve' history. But recently, these models have been developed further through the re-contextualisation of the documentary enterprise through interventions in sound and image. In relation to sound, three

dominant approaches have occurred – the use of testimony (interview, confession, observation); the use of actuality (fragmentary records of accidental soundscapes, edited as impressionist narratives); and those that are reconfigured (vocal idioms matched with images that read against the meaning of what is being said).

In relation to the re-contextualisation of the image, there have been four key developments: the creation of virtual, evidential, reflexive and performative contexts. The virtual context is evident in works such as **Virtual History** where computer-generated faces are superimposed on real characters. Evidential contexts utilise animation to evidence statistical, empirical or technical research and authenticate a particular situation, such as in Red Vision's visual effects for **Hiroshima**. Reflexive contexts use animation to address and interrogate itself, such as in **McLaren's Narratives**. Performative contexts are best represented by veteran National Film Board of Canada visionary, Pierre Hébert, and his live-performance animation in works such as **Special Forces**.

Hébert notes: 'Like all the **Living Cinema** projects, **Special Forces**, had a strange and indirect trajectory where concerns of technique, meaning and aesthetics were intermingled. We first started with the idea of controlling both our music and video live processing softwares with game pads. It was simultaneously a technical idea that was going to generate a lot of programming work and a stage idea.

We are just staging ourselves as artists in the face of the disturbing things now happening in the world, and we are addressing the audiences at an ethical level.
Pierre Hébert

Naturally, we started to include computer games graphics and sound in our improvisations, and for a while it seemed that it was going to be a piece about gaming. But it was difficult to get a satisfying format for the piece. In August 2006, when the Israeli army started to bomb Lebanon, we felt that we could not let that pass and we decided to transform our uneasy piece into a commentary about the war in Lebanon. It seemed to us that it was totally in tune with our previous **Living Cinema** pieces. The following week we received an email inviting us to perform at the Irtijal Festival of Free Improvised Music in Beirut. The idea of doing the world premiere in Beirut gave a very strong focus to our work. It made it a very acute and emotionally intense way to be involved in the subject matter of a piece.'

Hébert insists: 'We are not doing propaganda work, we are not trying to convince anybody of any political ideas. It is not that we don't have political ideas. In a way we are just staging ourselves as artists who accept to be on the "razor blade" in face of the disturbing things now happening in the world, and we are addressing the audiences at an ethical level. In that sense, the fact that it is being performed live is important because it implies that it is never a closed discourse, but a proposal that is always dependent on how we are personally affected by the development of the world situation.' Hébert's particular signature style of 'drawing' live in this kind of animation performance remains fundamentally related to his preoccupations across his career.

'It all comes from my long practice of animation scratched directly on film. This is how I started in animation under the influence of Norman McLaren and Len Lye. When I began to wonder why that technique remained so central for me for such a long time, it became obvious that its crude graphic and dynamic quality, its totally marginal situation in relation to the legitimate use of cinema technology, and the fact that it was so physical were at the core of my particular style. They were the reasons why I started to perform live, scratched animation. Those three aspects (crude images and movements, technological illegitimacy, and – to use Len Lye's words – "the bodily stuff") continue to be central elements to my technical and aesthetic approach to my latest work with computers. It involves doing everything to keep the technological apparatus transparent, so that a very strong human and physical element remains visible at the centre of it. In other words, working against the shiny computer look that is usually praised, so that the automated processes are put in tension with the human experience that must be at the core of any art, and which is the profound basis of communication with the audience.'

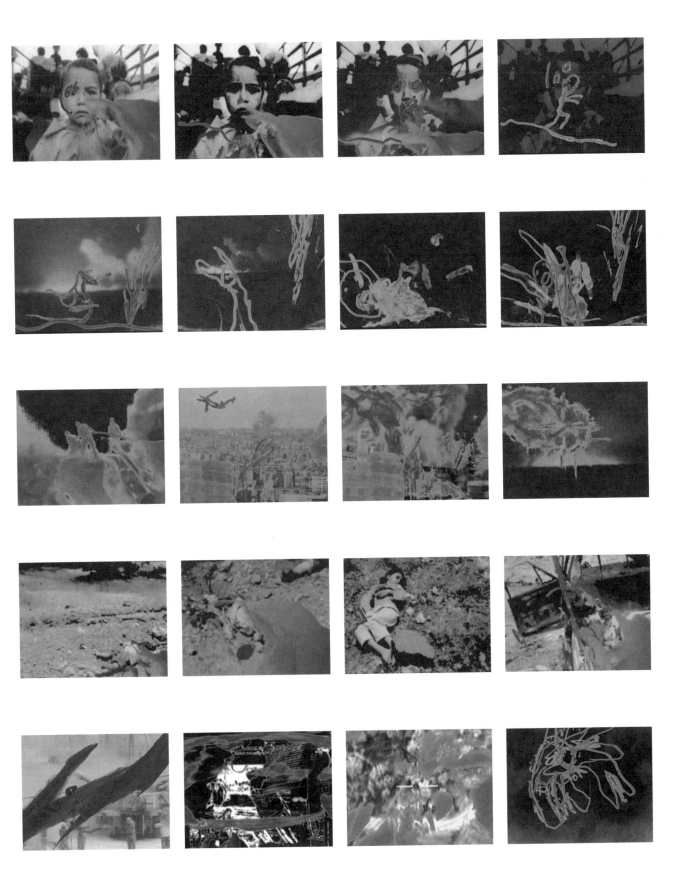

Pierre Hébert combines
images from news coverage
of the Israeli/Palestinian
conflict with hand-drawn
animated images performed
live on stage in order to
heighten the emotional
effect of fleeing children,
falling bombs and
indiscriminate brutality.

Hébert's response that he is pioneering a form of performative documentary takes up the idea that it is the language of animation itself that is at the heart of re-interrogating orthodox and taken-for-granted aspects of reality and its representation. He suggests that: 'The tradition in which I can situate myself is very marginal to mainstream character animation; it is constituted through a much smaller corpus of works. My basic interest is in how animation can relate to the real world and how it can relate to other types of images within a common and general relationship to reality.'

'My work certainly has to do with a documentary approach in a broad sense of the word. If I could express in an extreme fashion what my interest in animation is, I would say that I am more interested in what animation does to the perception of reality and to the perception of other types of images than in what it does just by itself. I am more fascinated by the effects it produces than in the worlds it creates. I should also add that the three stylistic elements I mentioned earlier are fundamental to this relationship to reality – the crudeness of graphics and movements, because it contradicts any phantasmagoric interpretation; the technological illegitimacy, because it questions the basis of cinema as a representation of the world; and the "bodily stuff", because having a strong feeling for the relationship between the animated images and the animating body is a fundamental and primary element of the relationship between animation and reality.'

'**Special Forces** includes a number of key motifs – a child's face, an abandoned doll, a missile and fleeing figures – which reflect the work's core political concerns: 'In developing the piece, we had many questions and uncertainties about the political ground on which we were standing, and also about what it meant to go to Lebanon and show the people who had suffered through it, images of their war. So finally we took what we may call a humanitarian rather than a political approach. . So the question of dead children (they were actually the majority of the casualties) seemed a good starting point and making the child's face a sort of witness of all the mess, became a good dramatic support for the improvisation.'

Work like Hébert's becomes a crucial tool not merely in the contexts of art, performance and animation – all areas that reflect his background and influences – but in education too. This work challenges and insists that the viewer recognises and interprets their own visceral responses, and engage with the ethical acceptability of the political, military and corporate agendas often underpinning conflicts based on the ideologies of faith and belief. This is a long way from the acceptance often encouraged in mainstream commercial work. Educators need to enable student cohorts to understand that the ennui and apathy that they experience in relation to all things political is often an intentional social construct. People are consistently encouraged to feel politically jaded and that all action is futile. There is a need to understand that this suits corporate interests and market stability perfectly. Hébert's stance, in person and through his work, resists this orthodoxy.

Gillian, the prostitute at the centre of Alex and Dave Beasley's animated documentary, **Revolving Door**, oscillates between a childlike naïvety and streetwise grittiness, captured in the tension between live action and animation in the film's aesthetic styling.

As in Marjut Rimminen's **Some Protection**, another example of 'subjective documentary', the fairground becomes a metaphor for legitimate fantasy and escapism, and an ironic orthodoxy set against the difficulties of street life.

Chapter 02   Authorship
                Attitudes and ethics
                Artist animation?

074/075

Education needs to lead its students in the urgent re-appropriation of such political and cultural history. In these circumstances, education clearly has a responsibility to nurture and empower instigators and initiators, not just to train cogs to work within one definition of a machine. Education should be empowering individuals, and part of that empowerment is for approaches such as 're-contextual documentary' to inform people about experiences outside their immediate knowledge and context.

RE-CONTEXTUAL DOCUMENTARY
—

Re-contextual documentary in this sense becomes an important educational model, taking up marginalised, dismissed or prejudged aspects of social existence, in order to promote 'the creative treatment of actuality' (John Grierson's original short definition of documentary) as a way of promoting new visual literacies, and thus to foreground significant social and cultural messages. If corporate and institutional culture fears mistakes and failure, this almost becomes the very subject of re-contextual documentary, which as the term suggests, repositions the argument or agenda of the particular issue. This is clearly the case in Dave and Alex Beasley's **Revolving Door**, a true account of what it was like to work the streets of St Kilda, Melbourne's red-light district. The film-makers hoped the production of the piece would provoke debate, discussion and, ultimately, social change.

Gillian is captured looking in the mirror - a clear metaphor for her confronting her own identity - as she considers her childhood and the feeling of abandonment she felt when taken into care. This led to her running away.

The Beasleys enjoy a playful reference to the fantasy idioms of B-movie street girls, which are a far cry from the realities of Gillian's unglamourous and painful existence.

A client cruises the St Kilda area, explaining why he is seeking out a prostitute and, in a casual manner, talks about the pleasures of unprotected sex and his fears of infection.

Initially, the piece was a conventional documentary shot over an extended period, utilising hand-held cameras to convey a sense of dynamism and energy in an attempt to capture and evoke the adrenalin of prostitutes working the streets. The capture of what the Beasleys describe as 'raw energy' was intrinsic to the idea of communicating lived experience and not an overly mediated view; it was their intention to use superimposed animated material on the live-action footage to suggest a range of thematic and conceptual perspectives. These include the idea that Gillian, the featured prostitute, may herself have actually drawn the frames, reflecting the naïvety of her understanding of her own experience.

Further, the use of colour on top of black-and-white footage contributes to a sense of artifice in the world; the animated and colourful once more representing Gillian's often innocent perception of a complex life. The animation also works as an effective mask to protect the identity and anonymity of the participants, which is crucial in the revelation of the often morally ambivalent, anxious, or oppressive activities of prostitutes, clients and police alike. The Beasleys add: 'We're not preaching to the converted – with such confrontational subject matter, animation is the perfect medium to soften the impact, giving the audience the choice of either enjoying the visual ride or immersing themselves in Gillian's world.'

The film also functions as a reaction to conventional, highly structured (and often quite static) computer-generated/assisted animation, and consequently uses the hand-drawn approach to reinforce its apparent immediacy and spontaneity. Crucially, the over-animating of live-action performance – here the real activity of a St Kilda sex worker – merely enhances the tragic circumstances of drug addiction, client indifference and brutality, and the social powerlessness of the street girls in the face of middle-class resident opposition.

The Beasleys recognise that the film itself is provocative and ethically engaged, so supported it with an extensive companion website: 'The companion website adds an entirely new dimension to Gillian's story. Again, it is meant to break away from traditional Web paradigms, attempting to build a site that is tactile, heuristic and open to the serendipitous, accidental discoveries. It also works as a powerful global marketing tool – especially amazing as we haven't really marketed the site and are averaging more than 500 hits per day, which has proven to us the awesome potential of the Web.'

The police become suspicious of Gillian and arrest her for prostituting herself.

We're not preaching to the converted – with such confrontational subject matter, animation is the perfect medium to soften the impact.
Alex and Dave Beasley

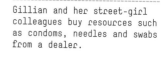

Gillian and her street-girl colleagues buy resources such as condoms, needles and swabs from a dealer.

Middle-class residents protest against the open presence of prostitutes in a well regarded residential area.

Gillian is beaten up by a client, but must continue her lonely life on the streets, unable to break the cycle of her addiction and her economic disadvantages.

The conscious use of cross-platform, related deliveries of animated artwork successfully extends the parameters of re-contextual documentary and enables the Beasleys to deploy animation as a subversive tool: 'Animation art is the best and sometimes only means of getting a political message across. The deceptive innocence of animation actually means the audience is more likely to be open-minded, particularly in today's political climate of fear and oppression.' Influenced by Maggie Fooke, the Melbourne-based animator, Ken Loach, the British left-wing film-maker, and Peter Greenaway, an artist/film-maker often concerned with layered screen aesthetics, the Beasleys wanted to engage with a hand-drawn rotoscope approach, which was definitely 'retro' as a deliberate reaction to the recent uber-clean computer-generated photorealistic work currently being pumped out.

This kind of approach deliberately sets out to challenge the thematic, aesthetic and technical assumptions of contemporary production, insisting that form properly service content and not merely operate as an arbitrary aesthetic. In being socially engaged and technically inventive without sacrificing impact or artistic ambition, **Revolving Door** points the way to a successful pedagogic model. This is teaching without preaching, insight without oversight. While the culture of digital animation technologies offers everyone a voice and implicitly encourages investment and experimentation, it is still the case that the most pertinent tools need to be chosen to facilitate an idea to its most enriching and revealing extent. Essentially, animation technologies offer individuals the opportunity to have a voice. Not only a voice, but also a proven, successful and effective voice. In so doing it is possible to level the social playing field, appropriate the aesthetics of industry, and to subvert and invert these visual language systems.

RESISTING CORPORATE AGENDAS

In a time when the creative dreams and visions of the individual are increasingly shaped by the capabilities, strengths and limitations of digital animation technologies, the Beasleys demonstrate that these tools can be used for challenging ends and outcomes. Where once the dreams and visions of practitioners led the development of CGI technologies, now CGI technology can shape human dreams and visions, and it is important that the software does not determine an approach. Arguably, corporate agendas can lie at the very heart of even the tools that we use to design, develop and deliver our work. Corporate culture provides, refines and sells tools, and it is crucial that animators and artists, as Hébert and the Beasleys have done, filter out corporate political doctrine from the visual and privilege personal work with integrity and challenge.

Chapter 02   Authorship   Art as politics, politics   078/079
                Attitudes and ethics   as art
                Artist animation?

ART AS POLITICS, POLITICS AS ART

In his piece, **Ask the Insects**, Steve Reinke develops the idea of manipulating and enhancing actuality footage in a more personal exploration, using animation not to focus on an observation of social conditions, but to chart the emotional experience of participating vicariously within social parameters.

He comments: '**Ask the Insects** started with a particular piece of footage. I videotaped with the camera resting on my shoulder as I walked the route I used to walk from my childhood home, through the northern Ontario village to the school I attended from kindergarten to grade eight. The school is on a hill. On the other side of the road is a graveyard that slopes down to a river. It was a summer afternoon and during the ten-minute walk the sky darkened ominously and a few drops of rain fell. I'd thought (and thought I remembered) my father was buried well into the graveyard, but when I got there I found that his grave was right next to the road, along with a slew of other headstones with our name.

'My work is often based on monologues told in the first person in which the narrator says things that might be personal. But these monologues, while they might have discursive or rhetorical similarities to confession or autobiography, never were. Often they were kind of meta-confessional or meta-autobiography. However, I did not see how I could do that with this footage. It was just too particularly, profoundly personal: walking through my hometown to my school and my father's

grave. Moreover, the power of the footage comes from its autobiographical nature: the fact that we end up with a bunch of headstones that all bear the name, the signature, of the author.'

ACTUALITY ANIMATION

Rather than seeking closure to the material through the imposition of a traditional narrative model, Reinke uses the material to interrogate aspects of what occurs when the image is manipulated, and how this might be understood as animation. The footage of the walk then becomes a series of introductions, false starts, gaps, interruptions, stoppages, this trip to the schoolyard that becomes instead a trip to the graveyard.

'The first thing I did was treat the footage with various digital filters. The colour is enhanced, but there are actually three layers of footage, each jittering at different rates, superimposed on one another with various types of keying and mode changes. Of course, almost all digital video, whether documentary or not, is colour-corrected and filtered in various ways, but I was trying to be more expressionistic. As well, the jitter in the images suggests a certain instability of time and event. So one could argue that even this piece of highly indexical, documentary footage is kind of an animation.'

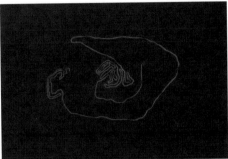

Reinke, a theorist of contemporary approaches to artist-led manipulated moving image[1], as well as an established practitioner, continues to work with the footage in a formalist manner: 'It was partly in order to argue that orthodox photorealistic images could be seen as animation that I made each of the eight or nine little sections that precede it a different type of animation. They're mostly done with After Effects, so they're not different types of animation in the sense of stop-motion or cel, for example. They're different types of animation in that they propose different relations between the "real" photographic world and the imagined-constructed-animated one.

'One of the sections is explicitly about animation. In it, I argue the opposite of what I've said above, that the abstract blobs one sees pulsing on the screen are not animation, but live-action footage digitally manipulated.' This deliberate challenge to image-making orthodoxy signals a change in the recognition and interpretation of animated forms, foregrounding two core image systems: the first is explicitly animation in a frame-by-frame, illusionist mode, predicated on now-established conventions of the cartoon, 3D stop-motion, new traditionalist CGI, collage and cut-out; the second is animation as a form predicated on revealing itself not through its own codes, but through manipulation, composition and collision with other image-making approaches.

Reinke feels that: 'A work in the first category cannot have anything to say about animation: it is too busy saying something through animation. Hybridised or messy meta-works can say something

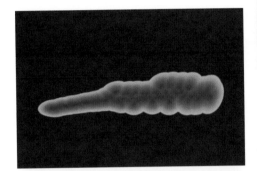

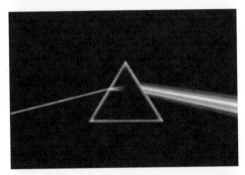

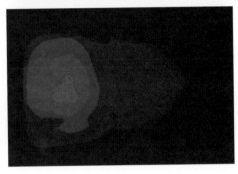

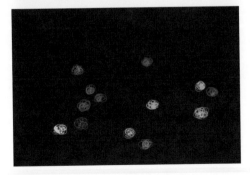

Reinke plays with various idioms of animation, ranging from the classical Disney style to scratching on film. This suggests the mutability of the image as a model by which shifting thoughts, emotions and perceptions might be understood. Reinke toys with well-known iconography and dissembling forms, challenging the audience to engage with shifting registers of reality and fantasy.

Chapter 02   Authorship   Art as politics, politics   080/081
                  Attitudes and ethics   as art
                  Artist animation?

about animation because it is not clear what they are generically. In the one case, one forgets that one is watching animation while, in the other, one just does not know if they are watching animation.' This tension is at the heart of a 're-imagining' of animation because it simultaneously acknowledges the established, if various, characteristics of established notions of animation, while using the very tools and approaches that create it to engage with other image forms as a way of interrogating and extending its vocabulary and achievement.

Reinke focuses on the challenge that underpins this re-imagining: 'I find images strange things. When I use language, I have a pretty good idea of what I'm saying or trying to say. And people listening to me know that the words are coming from me and, fairly often, what I mean by them and why I am saying them. So, while speech always has a speaker, and the meaning of the speech is largely determined by the relationship between the content of the language and the possible intentions of the speaker, images can exist freely. They are not spoken. As an artist who works with making meaning through combining speech and image, I find this quality of images confounding. Animation gives me a way to speak images, to use images rhetorically, and to unmoor photographic images from their referents. I don't want to turn image to language, I just want the possibility of deploying images rhetorically. I find this force that renders text visual and images textual very powerful.'

Animation has always been a self-reflexive language of expression, foregrounding its own codes and conventions. However, the digital shift in which creative practitioners find themselves using the same tools, has further complicated the vocabulary by which animation might be perceived and understood. Reinke's notion of the rhetorical is an important extension to the self-reflexive because it refers to the impact of other image systems and approaches to visualisation upon traditional animated forms, and facilitates a way in which they might be critically recognised and engaged with.

Interestingly, this might incorporate everything Reinke cites as his favourites, from Winsor McCay's **The Sinking of the Lusitania**, through to Alfred Hitchcock's **Spellbound**. Reinke makes an interesting observation: 'When animation reaches the art world, strange things happen. According to Rosalind Krauss (art critic and theorist), nothing happened between Disney and William Kentridge.'

At the heart of such an observation is the sense that animation is still effectively the art of slow, incremental development informed by a pro- or pre-filmic sensibility, and the conscious manipulation of form. The only real difference is the self-evident presence of the process itself, or its apparent absence. Re-imagining animation, then, inevitably becomes a stance, and one that is inherently political, with or without intent and intrinsically open to question as art or expression.

PERSONAL AS POLITICAL
—

Canadian video artist and teacher, Jan Peacock, has been drawn into debates about animation, through a questioning of her own practice and what she believed to be comparable work within her own discipline. She explains: 'For some time, I had been sick of seeing video projections and had a pressing awareness that I should stop making them myself – at least until they were no longer de rigueur in the art world. Trends like this produce habits of looking that are difficult to combat: perception levels out, is less articulate, active, and engaged. I like forms that freshly animate and energise involvement in looking – both maker and viewer.'

This idea of freshly animating chimes readily with Roland Barthes's engagement with Jean-Paul Sartre's perception of photography, where Sartre claims: '[C]ases occur where the photograph leaves me so indifferent that I do not even bother to see it "as an image". The photograph is vaguely constituted as an object, and the persons who figure there are certainly constituted as persons, but only because of their resemblance to human beings, without any special intention. They drift between the shores of perception, drifting between sign and image, without ever approaching either', which prompted Barthes to remark: 'In this glum desert, suddenly a specific photograph reaches me; it animates me, and I animate it. So that is how I must name the attraction which makes it exist: an animation.'[2]

Peacock wanted to take this sense of attraction as animation into the domestic environment and to reconfigure her approach: 'The Canadian Art Foundation asked me to make a work for their fundraising auction in Toronto.

I wondered what I could possibly do for someone at home that I would not be able to do for the same person in a museum. How to contend with scale and time, how to use light and darkness, movement and stillness, sound and silence, engagement and separation – everything would have to change in relation to the overriding intimacy and private experience of a home environment and the overlap of lives being lived there. With an audience of one family, how does one leave the public contexts and histories of video, relocating and re-describing it to be as intimate as these lives being lived together? This question led me to the work.'

For many viewers of the piece **Midnight Reader**, which features extensive sequences of a person's hand touching a range of domestic environments, there is a sense in which the person feeling the environment is an animator, who is in effect animating the space. The hand in essence becomes the tool of expression, replacing the pencil or brush, but in a certain sense foregrounding Hébert's sense of the 'bodily stuff' at the heart of the animation process. Peacock notes: 'That's completely congruent with my sense of the work. My original idea was to make a video drawing of the interior of a home, and this drawing would be one continuous line made out of touch and light. When installed, the video night-light object acts as a window that opens on to the temporal detail, the life of the house. Conversely, the house passes through that opening, via the recorded hand and the light that illuminates and guides the hand. This is animation in the figurative sense, too, as if the fingertips, in tracing the object or surface, make it luminous and retrieve it from darkness. It is important to keep in mind that all viewers outside of

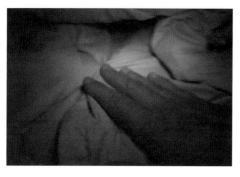

The fingertips exploring the surfaces of taken-for-granted household items and environments re-animate their presence.

Chapter 02   Authorship   Personal as political   082/083
              Attitudes and ethics
              Artist animation?

those who actually live in the house are secondary to the work. The house is deeply, but dormantly, animated for those who live there in embedded, unconscious ways. The fingertip tracing with light re-animates memory and experience that associate with individual histories of the viewer.'

This sense of the work echoes Jan Svankmajer's belief in the life entrapped in objects and environments, which the artist/animator effectively re-animates and releases. The presence of the hand also echoes any number of animations featuring the hand of a draughtsperson, painter or sculptor as it executes a work, but the absence of an artistic implement prompts the idea of a universal animus played out through the hand and a metaphoric suggestion of the difficulty in defining animation in the contemporary era.

With the 'digital shift', 'animation' has now become a complex term with a number of possible meanings for animators themselves. Peacock adds: 'Animation has become a hugely expanded field that seems to touch on everything – this has happened with design as well. And, because of our shared digital tools, all the fields are now in deep overlap, to such an extent that the categories are no longer descriptive. How do you separate video from film from design from animation? I rely on having lived and worked through a certain amount of their history as separate practices to understand how their specific and distinct cultural trajectories have converged and blurred, but my students don't have those histories and so don't make those distinctions. Animation, broadly, is shaping time, shaping events in time so as to reinvent our experience.'

Peacock's comment about current students not differentiating between applications and technologies is pertinent in the sense that in not seeing the differentiation between platforms, it is almost inevitable that there will not be a differentiation in discipline, nor any specific recognition that a discipline has a history and a relationship to cultural history. Crucially, these histories and applications need to be recovered and their significance addressed, not least of which, in a spirit of affinity and disparity. This may also be partly achieved through the proper engagement with artistic influences, and the role and function they play in helping to delineate the character of particular kinds of animation.

Peacock stresses: 'I pay a lot of attention to artists who concentrate on structures of time and language. I don't think so much about influences, but I have sometimes found affinities. I would say that the way Bill Viola handled editing in his early work shaped events in time in a way that is very close to my thinking – that temporality itself is available, malleable, up for grabs in the metaphysical and phenomenological senses and through technical experimentation, for a simple reason: we have such limited articulations of our experiences and consciousness of time, that there is only hypothesis and experimentation.'

According to Jan Peacock: 'The aesthetic aim of the night-light object is silence and unobtrusiveness; it is a small luminous surface embedded in a wall, flush with the wall's surface, as if maintaining contact with the skin of the house. It is situated in a place of passage (stairwell, hallway, foyer) so that it can guide one's movement, and so that one is always coming upon it with surprise. In spite of the smallness and silence of the object, there comes that little shock of recognising where in the house the hand is at the moment you find it, sometimes followed by a moment of puzzlement. For those who are living with **Midnight Reader,** the locating becomes more difficult as the landscape of the house changes over months and years.'

REFERENCES
1. Chris Gehman & Steve Reinke,
   **The Sharpest Point –
   Animation at the End
   of Cinema,** Ottawa:
   YYZ Books, 2005
2. Roland Barthes,
   Camera Lucida, London:
   Flamingo, 1984
   pp42-60

ARTIST ANIMATION?

—

The term 'artist animation' has gained currency in recent years. On the one hand, it is a term that seeks to differentiate between fine artists working in animation, and traditional animators; on the other hand, it is a potentially divisive and elitist term, coined in arts cultures, which effectively denies the recognition of an artist working in traditional, especially cartoonal forms.

In a field that has produced such major figures as Norman McLaren, Lotte Reiniger, Yuri Norstein, Chuck Jones, Hayao Miyazaki, Caroline Leaf, Nick Park, Paul Driessen, Joanna Quinn, Dusan Vukotic, Osamu Tezuka, Jan Svankmajer, John Lasseter and Frédéric Back, to deny them the epithet 'artist', would be churlish. In a more progressive and positive sense, though, the term points to the desire to elevate animation as a fine art practice, and to see it as a pertinent language in the pursuit of highly personal artistic goals, and for exhibition in contexts outside the broadcast and theatrical domain. There is a further implication that animation may be a highly pertinent tool in creating distinctive worlds rather than distinctive texts in themselves. Although virtually all the artists and animators discussed in this book have created 'worlds', this highly specific concept will be pursued in the following examples.

ARTIS
ANIMA

—
—
—
—
—

KEYWORDS IN THIS SECTION

Cartoon
This is one of the most difficult
things for artists and the commercial
sector to talk about. There is seemingly
something pejorative in the term for those
who might consider it the lowest form of
animation, intrinsically bound up with
character animation and gags. The cartoon
is simply a formulation in animation;
it can be as artistic as any other
approach, form or technique.

Manipulated moving image
The phrase 'manipulated moving image' has
been posited as a definition of current
animation practice, challenging the
conventional notion of frame-by-frame
animated film, with a view that the image now
possesses a higher degree of constructed-ness
through layering, compositing and mixed-media
composition. The term was suggested to more
properly embrace animated artworks, but
equally, it describes all aspects of post-
production and visual effects in mainstream
cinema. This may readily prove the elision
between live action and animation in the
creation of contemporary film-making, but
it does not fully recognise the distinctive
language of animation set against the
conventional nature of 'live action'.
Furthermore, it misrepresents the rhetorical
specificity of animation by immersing it
within the broad parameters of moving
image creation.

The term 'artist an
currency in recent
it is a term that se
between fine artis
and traditional ani
it is a potentially d
coined in arts cultu
denies the recogni
in traditional, espe
      In
such major figures
Reiniger, Yuri Nors
Miyazaki, Caroline
Driessen, Joanna C
Osamu Tezuka, Ja
Lasseter and Fréde
epithet 'artist', wo
progressive and po
term points to the
as a fine art practi
pertinent language

ALTERNATIVE
WORLDS I

—

The animation installation inevitably attempts to define a space as a unique territory; a small world particular to an artist, but an environment seeking out empathy and common bonds. The status of the animation within it may be various and challenging. It is sometimes the case that when a fine artist uses animation to make a point, the technical execution when compared to professional animators working in animated features may be seen as flawed, or indeed, merely making a point that has been made hundreds of times over in a range of cartoons in a gallery. Context, in this spirit, is all. This is especially the case with works explicitly working through humour – a gallery joke is 'wit' (by implication clever and insightful); a cartoon comic event merely a 'gag' (by implication potentially vulgar and excessive). While Zilla Leutenegger's animated cleaning lady signifies the disempowerment of women, Tex Avery's effacement and exaggeration of bodies in a variety of social scenarios, is 'just for laughs'.

Essentially, these approaches are the same and merely differentiated by cultures, contexts and critical communities. Recognition of intention, purpose and outcome is fundamental to the understanding of the nature of any art, but is particularly important if the fragmentation of animation cultures is not to undermine the work created in them. These 'ways of seeing' are ultimately the subject and object of artist animation.

Greg Barsamian's installation, **No, Never Alone**, was inspired by a Christian spiritual song bearing the same title. In addressing ways of seeing, Barsamian notes: 'The premise of the piece is intentional blindness. We are, above all, filter mechanisms. But the filtering required for faith is particularly intense. The images are a subconscious response to the intentional blindness required in true belief. The work is viewed as a free-standing sculpture. Darkness is required for the animation technique to succeed. The technique derives from pre-cinematic devices such as the zoetrope. A strobe light replaces the slits found in original devices. As each sequentially formed sculpture passes, the strobe light flashes giving your eye an image. Image after image, at a rate of ten per second, they are built by the mind into the illusion of motion much like a flipbook.

'As a sculptor I've always been enamoured by complexity, with the provision that all parts are necessary and all parts create "organic unity", or work toward a common goal. Equipping sculptures with the dimension of time greatly enhances the potential complexity of an otherwise static medium. This is not to say that time does not play a role in traditional sculpture. As a person walks around a sculpture, the two-dimensional image in our minds is like an animation. The shape changes wildly as we move about. Control of that animation is partly under the control of the viewer, however, and I am interested in controlling it more completely.'

Animation conjures up a huge variety of purposes and goals. As a tool it is near its ripened stage. It is now possible to create almost any image you can imagine with startling fidelity. As a tool for subconscious imagery it is ideal.
Greg Barsamian

This need for a sense of complete control is common to most animators and chimes with a need to create a particular world that reflects their own preoccupations, memories and level of consciousness. Barsamian seeks to render his piece not merely as a literal catalyst for perception, but a state of consciousness in its own right: 'The darkened room also aids my purpose. The creaks, clicking of the strobe and its flickering all help to create a subconscious-like atmosphere. That is something central to my work. Studies in information theory and cognition credit the conscious mind with operating at about the speed of language, that is, 15 bits per second. At the same time our senses are bringing in 20 million bits per second.

'Consciousness filters out the vast majority and in its chauvinism thinks otherwise. It sits beside a mile-wide river of information, dips a finger in here and there, and claims to know what is happening in the river. Worse, it often claims to be in control of the river! We're treated to bits of the expanded flow in flashes of insight, hunches, emotions and, of course, our dreams. It's for that reason that I've recorded my dreams for many years, culling them for bits of insight that smack of universality. The fodder for this gristmill is a subconscious and conscious reaction to my world; the political, social and emotional content of my experience. The language I work in is that of the subconscious.'

INTERIOR STATES
—

Animation's intrinsic capacity to capture and facilitate the representation of interior states of mind – memories, dreams, fantasies, solipsistic preoccupation – has been embraced throughout its history. As Barsamian notes: 'Animation conjures up a huge variety of purposes and goals. As a tool it is near its ripened stage. It is now possible to create almost any image you can imagine with startling fidelity. As a tool for subconscious imagery it is ideal. This is one of the qualities of the technique that drew me to it as a sculptor. Adapting it to three-dimensional objects was a way to marry the two. Combined with my "suburban motorhead" upbringing, it allowed me to add the dimension of time to sculpted objects while satisfying my internal need to get dirty and make things. As an illusion, the technique is a compelling one. Animating a three-dimensional object in real time and space suspends the disbelief and creates a tension reminiscent of dreams. The conscious mind wants order. It can find order in almost anything. It is the nature of that order that defines us. But we must remember that our experience viewed from any one angle is incomplete and viewed from all angles is incoherent. I do not offer order. Instead I offer the world of the unconscious where the emotions run wild and self-deception is an oxymoron.'

Barsamian's alternative 'world', then, is ironically the one we experience all the time, but have little understanding of, until such works offer empathy and insight.

The palpable sense of self-imposed claustrophobia, or externally determined oppression, is a consequence of unconditional investment in Barsamian's challenging installation - a metaphoric fabrication of solipsistic consciousness.

ALTERNATIVE WORLDS II

—

If Barsamian's world is essentially a perpetual present, a constant interrogation of consciousness-in-the-moment, then Joanna Priestley's installation work is more determinedly erected on the premises of the past.

PRIESTLEY AND PLAY
—

Extended Play is an experimental exploration and rediscovery of youthful preoccupations. It is set within the spotlight of an elliptical border, games, diagrams and objects of amusement to create an evocative metaphor of childhood pastimes. Arguably, play is at the heart of the animated form and is recovered through the processes of creativity.

Priestley has clear views on this: 'Children love play. As we age, we become encrusted with responsibilities, obligations, lists and schedules. We forget how to play. We leave playing to the professionals! We call them artists and pro-athletes. Isn't that ridiculous? Everyone should play. Everyone should make art. Everyone should enjoy sports and games. My best friend is phenomenally creative, but she refuses to make images or objects. She thinks that is only for professional artists! I love animating and find it playful in an obsessive kind of way. There are types of animation that I do not find playful, like lip-synching or filling hundreds of shapes with colour, but for the most part, I thoroughly enjoy it. If animation wasn't fun, no one would do it because it is so complicated to master.'

One of the most compelling frontiers is the animation of human beings in commercial feature films. There are new advances in the animation of human figures every year and pretty soon they will look real.
Joanna Priestley

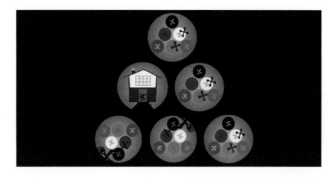

Joanna Priestley combines the icons and idioms of childhood play with the innovation of circular frames, which echo ball games too.

This sense of fun, coupled with a particular compulsion to address play as a conscious activity that takes place in real time, in real locations led to the development of her piece. Priestley explains: 'I began experimenting and playing with images in 2006 while working on the sound for **Streetcar Named Perspire**. It took a year to create the soundtrack and as the months wore on, I became fidgety. As a counterbalance, I started experimenting with shapes and colours in Flash and decided to stop working whenever it ceased being playful. I researched the iconography of play and games. It was a totally experimental process, free of the structure and goals of film-making.

'After six months of play, I reluctantly put the animation aside and moved on to a new film. Two months later, Marilyn Zornado asked me to submit a proposal for an installation for the Platform International Animation Festival. I brought out the play experiments and realised that most of the images were in a circular format. I designed a storyboard for Platform with image balls and ovals that moved around two perpendicular walls. My goal was to create an installation that was completely playful, one that expressed a clear sense of play to the viewer.

'I reworked the animation over the next five months and began collaborating with digital effects artist, Daniel Phillip Johnson. He reformatted everything, multiplied images and created interesting transitions and new compositions. **Extended Play** was designed for two perpendicular walls, so animated elements could change shape while moving across

the transition between the walls, and to create tension between the intersection of perpendicular elements. The entire piece was designed as a loop that would play continuously as pedestrians passed along the corner sidewalk. Several weeks before the premiere, we learned that budget constraints limited us to one projector. We switched from two walls to one. One week before the premiere, I produced a soundtrack with vocal artists Janet Day and Shannon Day (mother and daughter) and vocal sound effects wizards Sam Mowry and Martin Gallagher. Marc Rose added core sound effects and designed and created the mix two days before the opening. Every step of the process was play.

'It rained the night of the opening and we scrambled to move **Extended Play** inside. This part was not playful. We moved to a strange, second storey, computer lounge that had huge paper balls for lights. Perfect! We dimmed the lights and put gels in the paper balls to reflect the circular format of the installation. Mowry and Gallagher performed sound effects live as part of the installation, using voice, bicycle, coins, cards, balloons, drum, basketball and light sticks.'

Priestley's engagement with play, and the continual improvisation and adaptation that characterised this process – itself echoing the imitative and transformative qualities of children's play activities – speaks directly to both the mutability of the language of animation and the contexts it has traditionally been placed within.

PLAY AND DISPLAY

—

Priestley's aesthetic flexibility engages with this idea by working through different geometric compositions and contexts for display: 'My entire 18-film career has been contained in a rectangular format. It was very exciting to break out of that and create animation in a circle. This presented challenges, since our eyes are accustomed to seeing geometric, centred shapes within circles; quadrangular compositional rules do not apply. It was fascinating to work in a long thin format on a wall measuring 48 feet by 13 feet. I found that many separate, little movies could co-exist. It's much easier to be playful with that much space. Doing this project opened up my thinking about what animation can become. I would like to try new installation experiments with multiple projectors and props. Knowing that **Extended Play** would be seen outside in my own neighbourhood, I felt free to experiment with content, composition and structure. I wouldn't show it in a theatre, but might include it as a bonus item on a DVD now that some people have huge home screens and enough projection resolution to see the detail in the animation.'

Priestley, recognised as an experimental film-maker within the field of animation, has a broad vision of what this field constitutes and is in some ways skeptical about the delineation of 'artist animation' as a separate category, in that this could misrepresent what might be viewed as actually progressive in the form.

Priestley uses the opportunity to feature iconographic shapes and forms from children's games to create a formalist aesthetic, playing with the geometric and colourful as both art and play constructs.

NEW FRONTIERS?
—

Priestley notes that: 'One of the most compelling frontiers is the animation of human beings in commercial feature films. A few years ago it became possible to integrate realistic animation into live action in such a way that the viewer could not tell what was animated. There are new advances in the animation of human figures every year and pretty soon they will look real. People are creating huge motion-capture libraries for animating nearly infinite varieties of movement and combining multiple mo-cap sequences for variety. Now there are programs for realistic skin transparency and translucency. If only they could make the ankles bend and the eyes twinkle properly.

'The Platform Installation Festival in 2007 was a wondrous, three-ring circus, but did not feel cutting edge because some of the pieces were a decade old. There are so many different frontiers that people are working on now that nothing feels avant-garde. Three years ago, teeny, squawking animated movies on phone screens were cutting edge. Eight years ago, websites with gritty, interactive, animated narratives felt cutting edge. Showing animation out of the back of a truck to prevent AIDS in Pakistani street kids was avant-garde 20 years ago, as was combining animation with performance in the mid-80s. Abstract animation was avant-garde 75 years ago, and now many new abstract films are released each year. Cartoons made by individuals with great passion and unique vision can inspire creativity in viewers. That's the edge I love.'

Priestley's comments merely confirm that animation has consistently re-imagined itself and her crucial perspective on producing and showing work that inspires others, is surely at the heart of how educators, scholars and practitioners ensure yet further re-imagining.

Cartoons made by individuals with great passion and unique vision can inspire creativity in viewers. That's the edge I love.
Joanna Priestley

ANIMATION RE-IMAGINED

—

—

03

AN
RE-

0

RE-ANIMATING
HISTORY

—

It is important to recognise that the alternative worlds discussed in the previous sections, whether personal or social, have worked as interrogative interventions into assumed or taken-for-granted realities. Animators and artists realise that save for nature, there is nothing within our virtual/real culture that cannot be defined as in some way graphic.

Animation and design have become the natural state of artifice that we exist within. Our every waking moment is bathed in its light. Aesthetically triggered semiotic systems sway our every judgement, our every decision. We are continually directed and manipulated, increasingly ceding control of our lives to an external confident authority of mood, colour, message and tone. Design, predicated in static or moving image forms, has been so deeply absorbed into the contemporary consciousness that it is hard to recognise the myriad ways in which it stimulates, challenges, pleasures and angers. Its 'naturalisation' is part of Priestley's claim that it is difficult to identify an avant-garde. Our dreams, ambitions and memories are inextricably bound up with the perceived values that have been shaped, honed, packaged and sensitively delivered through commercial idioms, which in themselves have often absorbed the avant-garde as the new mainstream.

More importantly, our dreams, ambitions and memories are sometimes dangerously embedded in the attractions of CGI technologies and media that record our dreams, engender our desires and store our memories. Therefore, it is not unnatural for us to want to exist in and through alternative worlds. Such worlds inevitably draw upon the intrinsically metaphorical and metaphysical nature of animation as a language, and revise the perception of existence in order to get a better understanding of it.

Arguably, some of these worlds are escapist or banal, and a prerequisite for the creation of a more successful notion of the alternative is to suggest what an original vision is an alternative to. When an artist claims to be ironic, it surely begs the question 'Ironic about what?'. Further, in making these worlds available, animators are suggesting feelings and ideas that are often difficult to articulate, offering other kinds of experience. Ironically, this might yet tap into a more common experience that has been beyond the viewer to comprehend or understand, but which is recognised and understood through the empathy the work has foregrounded.

Chapter 03   —
              Re-animating history
              Re-defining practice
              Re-thinking artists

              —
              094/095

RE-AN
HISTO

—

—
—
—
—
—

KEYWORDS IN THIS SECTION

Visual literacy
Much is stressed in educational contexts
about traditional notions of literacy -
the written form, reading literary texts,
understanding language, etc. It remains
vital in the contemporary era, however,
to place much greater stress, much earlier,
on visual literacy. The ability to read and
understand images is a fundamental aspect
of understanding the media, art and politics
in the modern world, and animation can be
used as a ready vehicle to promote and
illustrate its significance.

Historiography
There are many ways in which history has been
written and constructed. The primary sources
which were once the most valued aspect of
writing the narratives of history -
statistical records, legal and social
documents, investigation of artefacts, etc -
are being replaced by the records of the
mass media, thus significantly altering the
demands and complexities of developing
authoritative historiography. This therefore
allows a much more relative, subjective,
counterfactual and personal view of history
to characterise current practices.

It is important t
alternative worl
sections, wheth
worked as interr
assumed or take
Animators and a
nature, there is
culture that can
way graphic.

become the natu
exist within. Our
bathed in its ligh
semiotic systems
our every decisio
directed and mar
control of our live
authority of moo
Design, predicate
forms, has been s
contemporary co
to recognise the
stimulates, challe
Its 'naturalisatio
that it is difficult
Our dreams, ambi
inextricably boun
values that have
packaged and sen
commercial idiom
have often absorb
the new mainstre.

03

VIRTUAL EXISTENCE

—

Animators and designers, due to their immersion in technology, are accustomed to and more accepting of the notion of 'virtual existence'. They flit between realities within their daily existence via platforms such as the Web, television, computer gaming and the media. As creators, they understand and adhere to one singular virtual truth in particular – if you can imagine it, then it exists. The phenomenon of animators creating their own worlds seems entirely natural. These alternate worlds are built from the virtual matter of global cultural references, of shared childhood media history and social history. They are idiosyncratic in the extreme, but globally understood.

Within the figure of the avatar in **Second Life** we could arguably see a distinctly political attempt to escape from real yet seemingly dead lives that are characterised by a desire to achieve an unattainable lifestyle. **Second Life** deals expressly in animating oneself, or even in re-animating oneself. One could argue that this is a bid to make good life's injustice and disappointment, or indeed a second chance at freedom and choice without consequence. However, what once constituted an escape has increasingly become a secondary capitalist market, a corporate industry recognising that it can ostensibly operate on a secondary level through virtual trade and promotion.

It is crucial that such spaces are not colonised wholly in this way and that animators and artists do not create a replacement reality complicit with this model. The explosive widening of the discipline should not simply be about escapism in its most benign form, or in globally troubled times, a bid to elude the trans-generational transmission of trauma. It is also important that work does not attempt to comfort the self through the construction of mere stability, less a political stance than a metaphorical foetal position.

The generation of new idylls might authenticate and legitimise a new, virtual existence in an increasingly fragmented society, and there is a danger that animated films are simply an aide-memoire to artificial memories, in some way aimed at making real what is perceived and what might ultimately be illusory. Imagined worlds should not be an attempt to keep the real world at a safe distance and should embrace the complexity of relationships, and the genuine impact of the social and political. Although many animators enjoy the control that animation gives them and the worlds they can create with it, many, indeed most, are characterised by a common sense of social responsibility and an almost utopian vision of the benefits that film and design can bestow.

Chapter 03   Re-animating history   Virtual history   096/097
               Re-defining practice
               Re-thinking artists

VIRTUAL HISTORY

—

CONSPIRACY AND CONFRONTATION
—

Conspiracy theories rage about some of the major world events of the modern era – most particularly, the Kennedy assassination and the events of 9/11 – fuelled by the proven criminal complicity and corruption of Watergate, which has encouraged the view that all political action is open to mistrust and challenge. This is in some ways inevitable and perhaps evidence that public doubt and scepticism are ironically barometers of a progressive democratic spirit. Animators and artists working with these ideas may face greater risks by engaging with some of the 'sacred cows' of major incidents – offence to the grieving, potential disrespect for the dead, challenge to government and God, or scepticism about racial or religious ideologies.

In recent years, one of the most ethically challenging animated films in this regard is Edouard Salier's **Flesh**. Here, the principal events of 9/11 are presented as the consequence of a self-indulgent, hedonistic America, and the attacks themselves are played out like computer games on skyscrapers and public dwellings alike, and are covered in pornographic images. Salier explains: '**Flesh** is the second volume of a two-film series about the American Empire. The first one is called **Empire**, which I made when George W. Bush was re-elected in October 2004. First of all, I did not want to make a simple-minded anti-American film, because I am coming from the generation that has grown up with American culture. **Empire** points a finger at the US political system and superimposes two sides of the American myth: the transparent war force, almost invisible, finds itself embedded in images of a quasi-advertisement-like bliss. **Empire** is therefore a graphic illustration of the American way of life and of its war-mongering background. The key questions remain: Does the American way of life only exist because of the military force of its army? Are prosperity and comfort necessarily bound up with the force of the US military strike force and models like it?

'**Flesh** is based on a visual principle that is the contrary to the one explored in **Empire**: the buildings of a megalopolis are covered in images from porn films. Several ideas are intertwined in the surfaces of which the town is made. The images of an idealised American life are replaced by images of sensual and shameless women, while the warlike imagery, usually imagined through fighters and tanks in foreign cities, is replaced by American architectural structures attacked by airliners. Those attacks have finally no effect on the town; on the contrary, they only increase the spectacular decadence they are trying to knock down. The more the planes attack the town, the more debauchery, gigantism and violence proliferated. Whereas **Empire** illustrated American violence as a foundation for supposedly protecting family and economical values, **Flesh** explores the hypocrisy in America, which pretends to be modest and moral, but is in fact immensely violent and decadent.'

Edouard Salier's controversial **Flesh** creates an American city environment covered with provocative images from pornographic films. It signifies the decadence and self-indulgence of American culture, and implies that the loss of life during 9/11 was especially wasteful.

Salier's approach favours a mix between the glossy aesthetics of news spectacle, the soft focus of hardcore erotica, the often harsh, sub-animated action of the computer game, and the hand-held feel of amateur vérité – a potpourri of contemporary reality stylings that at once evoke popular cultural forms, but foreground their fantastical representational feel. Computer animation and visual effects readily service this uncertain yet profoundly recognisable space.

Salier notes: 'The sets and planes have been modelled, animated and textured; we used stock shots for the "virgins" video, and everything was composited on After Effects – very democratic tools you can use on a basic personal computer. **Flesh** is my first full 3D animation piece. The technique was always dictated by the material I wanted to develop. To create the visual style of the film we would have to work with 3D. It is clear that as a tool for new film-makers, the new technologies applied to animation can be used for more political statements, as artists can often create films alone. But I don't consider myself as an animation director or experimental director. It is very important to me to experiment, but not fundamental to my practice. I don't want to make experimentation at all costs. I try above all to communicate an emotion, a "message" or a feeling, no matter what the form, which imposes itself subsequently according to the meaning I want to convey. But if I manage to do it and develop original visual ideas at the same time, it is all the better.'

ETHICAL CONCERNS
—

At a recent conference at the Tate Modern, UK, ethical concerns were raised about **Flesh**, suggesting that bringing together pornography and the imagery of 9/11 was in some way unacceptable. Salier resists this view though: '**Flesh** is open to multiple readings and plays with the ambiguity of the two camps. It doesn't favour any side, but it doesn't let anyone off easily either. The text that opens the film contains a reference to the 70 virgins promised by recruiters as a reward to terrorists. Although this section of the Koran leads to confusion and obviously needs to be handled with care, its usage by the recruiters of suicide bombers is without a doubt abusive. One possible ironic reading of the film that justifies the visions of these naked girls is that it is a fantasy of a kamikaze before he hits the towers. Thus, the decadent West he intended to destroy is also a source of desire, one that is ironically encouraged by a religious fundamentalism that attacks the West, all the while playing on its attractions.'

It is this aspect of titillation, of course, which remains challenging – it can distract from, confuse, and render ideologically incoherent some of the themes in the film. What it does throw into relief, though, is the idea that America's fundamentalist, self-righteous extremism sits uneasily against the reality of an eight-billion-dollar-a-year porn industry, a ready metaphor for the excesses of corporate pleasure, excess and greed.

I don't consider myself as an animation director or experimental director. It is very important to me to experiment but not fundamental to my practice.
Edouard Salier

Chapter 03   Re-animating history   Virtual history   098/099
             Re-defining practice
             Re-thinking artists

Salier continues: 'The film compares and contrasts the Americans and the terrorists. America is as corrupt, libidinous and excessive as the religious fundamentalists present it. America, the superpower, is subject to the contradiction that it can bring fervour and energy to its convictions, and this can feed its aggression towards others, and yet it can contain within itself an inherent violence that is a challenge to the foundations of its very own empire. **Flesh** shows how the kamikaze planes fuelled the flames and stirred the arrogance and imperialist mindset of a superpower that is full of contradictions. The airliner attacks ultimately have no lasting effect on the city. On the contrary, they increase the spectacular decadence they are trying to destroy.'

The film does not intend to take sides for or against the United States or the Islamic fundamentalists – it is a reinterpretation of the events of 9/11 and their aftermath, which spurred on the reassertion of a superpower, enhanced its military supremacy and encouraged the spread of US hegemony. Accompanying this warlike rebirth comes the rising significance placed on domestic morals and puritanism, which, ironically, mirrors the radicalising of the fight by Islamic fundamentalists against the decadent West.

Salier's virtual history, subjective and complex as it is, insists upon knowledge of seemingly opposing cultures and an understanding that people from different backgrounds, disciplines, ideologies and prejudices need to rethink assumptions; in this, the language of animation as a re-imagining tool has become invaluable.

Salier's combination of 9/11 imagery and pornography is ethically and ideologically challenging, but it prompts what he views as a necessary debate about hidden and profound political agendas of late capitalism.

RE-CONTEXTUALISING HISTORY

—

Salier's film uses animation as a tool in the deliberate provocation of history – a 'what if?' scenario predicated not on projection, but on a 're-presentation' of the issues in the light of sometimes repressed or resisted perspectives. Animation also offers the possibility of a genuine 'what if?' scenario by enabling the creation of plausible reconstruction. Tiger Aspect Productions and The Moving Picture Company produced a documentary drama entitled **Virtual History: The Secret Plot to Kill Hitler**, which focuses on events that took place on the 20th of July, 1944. It follows the war leaders – Adolf Hitler, Sir Winston Churchill, Franklin D Roosevelt and Josef Stalin – as they take significant decisions in what will be the last phase of the War, including the plan to assassinate Hitler.

CONSTRUCTING HISTORY

—

The Moving Picture Company deployed computer animation techniques to combine treated live-action footage and specially constructed facial imaging. Their goal was based on historical documents and accounts, and to transform the faces of actors into exact replicas of the major protagonists and turn contemporary live-action material into authentic 1940s colour archive. The process used to recreate the political leaders involved the following main stages, which demonstrate the combination of traditional craft skills and digital imposition. Firstly, plaster casts were made of the actors' heads. A sculptor then used these as a base upon which to fashion realistic faces of the historical figures. Once the faces were complete, the busts were laser-scanned in order to create digital copies in the computer. The faces were then extracted from the heads and textured. During the live-action shoot, the actors wore specially designed rigs with markers, which allowed for the subsequent tracking of their heads in the footage, and the replacement of their faces with the computer-generated versions. The actors then repeated their lines in a facial motion-capture session. Their facial movements, including all dialogue and gestural expressions, were recorded and processed, and then applied to the computer-generated faces, bringing them to life and offering the possibility of re-animating and reconstructing historical events.

The fully textured digital faces were lit to match the on-set lighting conditions and then composited into the live-action footage. Once The Moving Picture Company team was content with the plausibility of the recreated leaders, digital grade and damage effects were added to the shots. In order to fully authenticate and emulate archive material, the team researched the properties of different film stocks of that period, and also created a probable 'life story' of the exposed film. Archive footage can potentially go through a complex history of changes in itself, subject to different kinds of storage, chemical deterioration, and the uses and abuses of ownership; so this was taken into account as part of the ways that modern technologies could imitate this. Likely American, German and British-film looks were created, each

Chapter 03   Re-animating history   Re-contextualising history   100/101
                    Re-defining practice
                    Re-thinking artists

displaying different colour slants and propensity to damage. The resulting archive footage closely matches those of the 1940s – presenting a mixture of conditions that echo the implicit history of archiving, as well as the historical events themselves.

PHOTOREALISM REVISITED
—

This attention to detail ultimately supports the idea of realism, which renders the imaginary events as if they were real. This significantly problematises the status not merely of documentary, but of any supposedly photorealistic record of a non-fictional event. It should be recognised, though, that photorealism, since the beginning of cinema and throughout the history of documentary forms, has never been a wholly trustworthy record of such events. It is subject to a variety of technical and mechanical interventions, and most importantly, the dictates and choices of authorship and the deliberate construction

of representational idioms. What is at stake, in the contemporary era, is the scale and degree of 'constructedness'. Pioneer documentarist, John Grierson, always accepted that documentary was concerned with the 'creative treatment of actuality', but in the case of the virtual history represented here, actuality is created for treatment; although based on thorough research and historiographic integrity, it nevertheless makes the animated imaginary the same as the proven real, and this significantly redefines all non-fiction-based work.

The Moving Picture Company combined the physical presence of a real actor, appended a computer-generated face to the original actor's head, and treated the footage to look like damaged archive material in their reconstruction of the attempted assassination of Adolf Hitler.

RE-DEFINING PARACTICE

John Finnegan, Associate Professor for Computer Graphics Technology at Purdue University College of Technology at New Albany, and his colleagues, Richard Kopp and Carley Augustine, recognised that it was important not only to engage with ideas about history and technology, but also to look at how art history might be able to facilitate a greater degree of recognition about the relationship between (animated) art and (computer) science.

Finnegan explains their project, **Modeling Art History: Exploring Edward Hopper's Nighthawks Outside and ... IN!**: 'The art history portion of this project was inspired by a number of factors in the creators' range of experience. Firstly, the creators came to computer graphics technology and to three-dimensional modelling and animation from the disciplines of theatre, fine art, graphic design and instructional/educational technology. The perception is that engineering and technology-focused curricula are not as likely to seek these resources. Liberal and fine arts programmes are by nature more inclusive of a broader range of topics than math, science and engineering-based programmes.

'The impetus for the specific content for these projects was inspired by Rutgers University's SIGGRAPH 2002 and 2003 Educator's presentations entitled **Animating Art History**. The team from Rutgers describes a process where animators and art historians come together and build tools-animated artworks that can be used to teach art history. The three-dimensional aspect of the tools developed adds a level of visualisation and appreciation that doesn't necessarily exist experientially in the original work, but can affect how a student views and perceives the work with these newly developed tools. Also, the animated Vermeer project from the SIGGRAPH Computer Animation Festival, created by Interface Media Group, Washington, DC, shows the painting, **The Music Lesson** by Johannes Vermeer, and this was influential. Using computer graphics tools and visualisation techniques, the Vermeer work was deconstructed to show changes made by the artist, and also allowed exploration of the space in which the painting subject exists. It added a thoroughly new appreciation for the work of this master, and how his process for a painting might change over the life of the process of creation.'

Chapter 03   Re-animating history
                  Re-defining practice
                  Re-thinking artists

102/103

**RE-DI
PRAC**

KEYWORDS IN THIS SECTION

Art history

Art history underpins approaches to animation
in a number of ways. Its achievements can
be the source of a visual styling. The
techniques and approaches undertaken by fine
artists can be used by animators; and the
images themselves can be used for formalist
experimentation, historical investigation
and technical knowledge.

Collaboration

Increasingly, there is clear recognition
of the role and function that collaborators
play in bringing their individual expertise
to the development of a project. Artists
may view their strengths in visualisation,
calling upon composers to add creatively
to the project. These kinds of collaborative
projects can function as experimental
research as well as creative outcomes.

John Finnegan,
Computer Grap
University Colle
Albany, and his
and Carley Aug
was important
about history ar
at how art histo
a greater degree
relationship bet
(computer) scie

project, **Modelir
Edward Hopper
and ... IN**!: 'The
project was insp
in the creators'
the creators can
technology and t
modelling and ar
of theatre, fine a
instructional/edu
The perception is
technology-focu
likely to seek the
and fine arts pro
more inclusive of
topics than math
based programm

03

ANIMATING NIGHTHAWKS
—

Finnegan chose Edward Hopper's realist masterpiece, **Nighthawks**, as the subject for his students to research and recreate as a three-dimensional animated space. The object was to create the diner in the painting and as much of the surrounding environment as possible with the ultimate goal of being able to enter the painting and the diner, and see what the subjects in the painting are seeing. **Nighthawks** was chosen for the architectural nature of the subject matter.

Finnegan notes: 'The students realised through analysis and discussion that they would have to include and model many items that weren't evident in the two-dimensional painting by Hopper. Once they realised that a viewer could come into the world of the painting and essentially enter at the diner, they should be able to see things such as the floor, the ceiling and behind the counter. This sparked their curiosity. Additional research and modelling was outlined and assigned and they continued production.'

Having viewed Hopper's original painting, the group felt even more invested in creating a highly authentic environment: 'It raised their internal expectations as they now had been in the presence of the original, and it mattered more that they get it right. The group even went so far as to photograph themselves in costume and composite themselves into the final rendering – a move that would make Marcel Duchamp smile.'

The Nighthawks project required us to extrapolate from data we could observe in Hopper's painting to data not visible in the painting. Using inference, or projection from 'what we know' to 'what we conjecture' is always a good learning process.
Jerry Banick

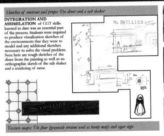
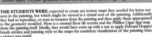

Notes and plans for the
re-animation of Nighthawks.

Chapter 03   Re-animating history
               Re-defining practice
               Re-thinking artists

104/105

This re-animation of the painting is essentially a re-imagining of its status as an artwork and its place as historical evidence about art, American culture and the relationship between the perception of the artist and the subject engaged with. For the students, it is an apposite approach to understanding the compositional and material difference between 2D and 3D, and most importantly, aesthetic concerns, when played out through the pragmatic nature of real and imagined environments in computer animation. Participating student Jerry Banick notes: 'The **Nighthawks** project required us to extrapolate from data we could observe in Hopper's painting to data not visible in the painting. It was necessary to infer things such as the possible look and texture of the diner's floor, the lighting fixtures and the backside of the counter. That type of thinking, using inference or projection from "what we know" to "what we conjecture" is always a good learning process.'

This process of conjecture is once more particularly enabled by the freedoms of the animated form, which intrinsically moves beyond both the confines of the real and the representational.

Video artist Anouk De Clercq uses a key historical source as an associative and symbolic prompt in her work, **Kernwasser Wunderland**: 'I had been fascinated by Prypyat and Chernobyl in particular for a very long time. The idea of an empty, deserted landscape, but one which is filled with a deadly presence and threat – radioactivity – that can't be seen, can't be touched, can't be smelt, but only heard through a Geiger-teller machine, seemed to me to be a good starting point for a project in which sound and image are the catalysts and stimuli for each other. My own creative energies were continually prompted by a personal experience related to my fascination for Chernobyl. A couple of years ago, I had to be treated for thyroid disease and they had to inject a radioactive kind of fluid in order to see the problem. My doctor told me that the rate of thyroid diseases was much higher since the Chernobyl disaster, and this merely developed my interest further.

'What we wanted to achieve was a video piece that evoked a world, but also a world in evolution, and you never know whether it is a positive evolution or a negative one. I always wanted to portray a reversed kind of Chernobyl in the sense that the landscape is at first empty; explosion and implosion occur, which changes the tones of the video (the constant play between black, white and greys) but in the end, something is growing in the landscape (the flower-like figures).'

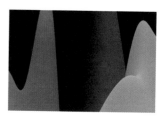

Anouk de Clercq's **Kernwasser Wunderland** creates a particular world that is part abstract and part suggestive of a decimated environment. Shapes and forms are half seen in the dust clouds, echoing the peaks and troughs of Geiger-counting instruments. These are combined with organic forms that are insistent and resistant to the effects of nuclear fallout.

HISTORICAL SOURCES
—

'Concerning the sound/image: we wanted neither of the two layers to be an illustration of the other. We wanted the two layers to play with each other; sometimes the sound takes the lead and moves the image forward, sometimes it is the image that asks the music to speak what it can't say.'

If the **Nighthawks** project invited students and subsequent viewers to interrogate a historical space through a virtual artwork, De Clercq wishes to engage with an implied historical condition through the use of a real gallery space. She notes: 'In a traditional screening venue you don't get to play with that other element: the space. Since 2002, I have been presenting my work in galleries or museums and this adds the possibility of creating a space for the images and sounds. This includes considering the colour of the walls, the seating element, how the place is designed, looking at the carpet on the floor, where the audience comes in, and the spatial qualities of sound. We have built a dark labyrinth where people had to find their way in the dark, with only the sounds of **Kernwasser Wunderland** to guide them. At the end of the labyrinth, there was a big projection of the piece on a specially designed screen.'

COLLABORATION
—

De Clercq recognises that even though this was a collaborative project in which artists are focused on developing a core concept, the digital animation technology became an important protagonist. 'We worked mostly online and rarely met. Eavesdropper sent us a couple of sound excerpts based on the Chernobyl subject. The computer and the animation program never stops surprising so you can't possibly work in a rigid way, I feel. The computer and the software is the fourth collaborator in this project. But anyway, Joris and I made the first three minutes of the piece, as the introduction to the landscape. We sent that to Eavesdropper so he could make the sound to it. Then Joris and I continued to work on the image. We didn't talk much, we sent each other images and sounds.'

Antennae revolves picking up signs of life, yet also presents an abstract shape in the void.

Chapter 03   Re-animating history   Reclaiming animation   106/107
             Re-defining practice   history I
             Re-thinking artists

RECLAIMING ANIMATION HISTORY I

Marie-Josée Saint-Pierre's **McLaren's Negatives** is an animated documentary about one of animation's most influential figures – Norman McLaren. His experimental works provide much of the foundation for the numerous approaches that are taken in the field even in the contemporary era. His interest in technology, technique and formal enquiry, all imbued with a political zeal about the value of animation as a democratic and expressive form, has prompted many artists to engage with their own work in a spirit of enquiry and artistic questioning. It is important to recognise McLaren as a key influence and to promote his legacy, but contemporary artists must also foreground his significance historically and aesthetically.

Saint-Pierre's work seeks to do this. She says: 'I discovered Norman McLaren when I was studying film animation at Concordia University in Montreal. I remember being introduced to his work and thought I had never seen anything quite so amazing. Norman McLaren is a singular artist who really has made paramount innovations in film-making. He is a true pioneer of frame-by-frame film-making. He made films using a very wide variety of techniques such as scratching, painting, ink, drawing, pixellation, and cut-outs. He even drew the sound directly on to the 35mm filmstrip! I think he is a genius and a film-maker who is worth talking about and seeing his films is a must for any lover of the seventh art. My personal favourites are **Neighbours** (an Oscar winner in 1953), **Blinkity Blank** (Palme d'or International Film Festival winner for Best Short Film in 1955), **Pas de Deux** and

Norman McLaren is a pioneer in experimental animated film, developing and exploring many unusual techniques. He still remains profoundly influential in the contemporary era.

Begone Dull Care. I wanted to make my film as homage to him. I also think he is not as known to the general public as he should be. The quality and scope of his work are truly exceptional.

'This film was made over several years. I started painting the backgrounds in 2001, so I guess it evolved with me and my film-making style. They were made with the 16mm film negative that was left from the first-struck print of my first film **Natural Selection**. After the final cut, I had so much film negative left and I could not stand having it go to waste. I started cutting the 16mm film negative with scissors in different shapes and sizes, and then I dyed it inside old, plastic soft-drink bottles. I then randomly painted and stained the film by letting the celluloid soak in these kaleidoscopic colour mixtures. After drying them, I then mounted the 16mm coloured filmstrips on transparent 35mm film, and these were scanned at a high resolution. Frames were then chosen to compose the background of the film. I wish I had more income as an independent artist so I could print some of the negative strips on giant light boxes. They would look amazing!'

Saint-Pierre's self-evident willingness to experiment and her approach to multiple techniques echo the formal experiments and diverse practices of Norman McLaren.

Saint-Pierre contextualises McLaren's achievement by referring to his Oscar for the anti-war parable, **Neighbours**.

Saint-Pierre uses one of McLaren's personal metaphors and motifs - the chicken - which appears in a number of his films. It is a symbol of the purely intuitive and the intrinsically 'animal'. It also conveys the sense of 'the other' that informs McLaren's instinctive investment in his formalist interrogations.

Jazz was a major influence on McLaren's abstract style. In high school, he claimed to interpret music through the visualisation of shapes, colours, lines and forms.

Chapter 03   Re-animating history
              Re-defining practice
              Re-thinking artists

Reclaiming animation
history I

108/109

MULTIPLE TECHNIQUES
—

'There are many techniques in **McLaren's Negatives**. There are traditional hand-drawn animations that were made by Brigitte Archambault. These hand-drawn animations are very dynamic and alive. There is also an important amount of rotoscope animation – a technique that consists of filming the action with a model, and then having the animator retrace the contour of the figure. These rotoscopic animations were then treated by the special effects artist, Kara Blake. She prepared mattes to create McLaren's dark silhouette. Other items in the film include: treated and animated photographs; hand-painted and drawn backgrounds, as well as McLaren's film clips.'

Saint-Pierre effectively collapses McLaren's techniques into one process, making the subjective interrogation of McLaren's art a model of understanding about how a contemporary artist has absorbed and reflected his influence. Her main intention, however, was not to essentially document McLaren, but to preserve and extend the notion of memory.

Many aspects of life are often forgotten and these reinventions or re-imaginings of people, lives, relationships, spaces, environments and experiences are effectively acts of remembering – new records of significant knowledge and practice, which are threatened with effacement by time. Animated virtual histories resist this process. Saint-Pierre, even by working with film, insists upon an act of preservation – film is treated as a physical material, handled like a sculptor's stone, or a furniture maker's piece of wood. **McLaren's Negatives** introduces a new generation to Norman McLaren and to the idea of traditional film-making, itself rapidly receding in the post-photographic era

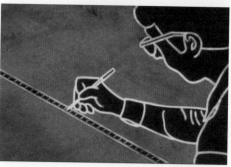

McLaren always drew a parallel with the practices of the fine artist and his own approach as a film-maker.

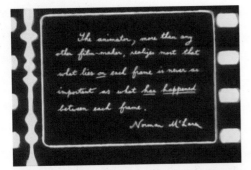

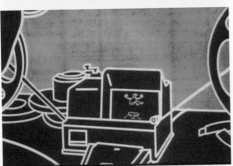

McLaren stressed that the thinking and decision-making process in the creation of images is more important than what was actually on the frame itself.

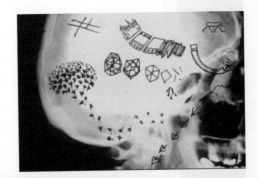

Saint-Pierre's work draws on another documentary, **Creative Process**, where McLaren tries to describe the thoughts that unfold in his mind while creating animation. Saint-Pierre celebrates McLaren's work and his sense of humility.

Chapter 03   Re-animating history   Reclaiming animation   110/111
              Re-defining practice   history I
              Re-thinking artists   Reclaiming animation history II

RECLAIMING ANIMATION HISTORY II

In Eric Dyer's **Copenhagen Cycles**, a cyclist travels through a fantastical, collaged reconstruction of Denmark's capital city. The combination of the pre-cinema zoetrope with fast-shutter digital video technology explores the kinetics of Copenhagen life and plays out an important relationship between proto-animation and post-photographic animation. It suggests that the hand-crafted processes of the pre-cinema era are directly echoed in the craft techniques of the contemporary animator using digital technologies. Dyer spent eight months in Copenhagen on a Fulbright Fellowship. He rode around on a bicycle to collect source footage of the city's moving elements, printed and cut the sequences, and then built around 25 cinetropes (zoetrope-like sculptures).

   Copenhagen Cycles is composed entirely of unprocessed shots of the spinning sculptures. Dyer describes working on the project: 'I wanted to work away from the computer screen, get back to physical processes, and also move animation away from flatness and into real space. I began by creating zoetrope-like sculptures registered with strobe lights, but was unhappy with the flickering effect of the strobe. I realised that using a fast shutter speed on a progressive scan DV camera could also register the sequence parts. This discovery was especially thrilling to me, because I'm a film-maker at heart and using this process means I could create installation art and make films.'

TRADITION AND MODERNITY
—

Dyer's working imperatives challenge the viewer to evaluate how the images are created. By operating as an installation, the work provides a visual parallel between traditional and new forms of animation – one creating and reflecting upon the other.

   'The **Copenhagen Cycles** installation is really an exposé of the process used to create the film of the same name. I find that audiences are very interested in how the film was created. Many think that the images are computer-generated and effected – when I tell them the film is composed of raw, unprocessed footage of the spinning cinetropes, they are amazed and become very curious about the process. It should not really matter to an audience how the film was made – it should stand on its own, regardless of process, but it seems we have already acquired a kind of quiet disinterest or disbelief in computer-generated work – it seems like it is only a trick – soulless. The reaction to **Copenhagen Cycles** made me really want to show the process, show the objects I created to make the film, and to show those objects in action, live. In the layout of the installation I made sure audiences encountered the live video feed of the spinning cinetropes (the animation) before revealing the process – an attempt to get the audience/viewer to question the process before understanding it.'

Eric Dyer creates cinetropes of images of Copenhagen, cutting out innumerable shots to mount on a three-dimensional zoetrope-style system.

—

Like Saint-Pierre, this kind of work recognises a lost aspect – not merely of animation and animation as an art, but of the very experience of engaging with animation as a form. Dyer adds: 'It is interesting to look at animation history and see how technologies heavily influenced the aesthetic of the works created. Today, one can sit in the cinema or in front of the TV and say, "that was created in Maya" or "that was created in After Effects", for example. Each piece of software and each tool system forms its own grammar through which we express ourselves. I am interested in creating with tool systems of my own design, to create new expressive frameworks.

'When motion picture film was invented, animation moved to the screen. Quickly forgotten were the zoetropes, phenakistascopes and praxinoscopes. That sort of animation was a tool system with its own grammar, one of loops and spirals and tactility. With the creation of **Copenhagen Cycles**, I have dug up that old grammar and re-explored its expressive potential. Thanks to the latest DV technology, I have also been able to bring it to the screen. Because of real-time, hand-held DV is used to 'see' the moving elements on the cinetropes; intuition and spontaneity also become part of the process, itself unusual for animation.'

Dyer's judicious use of contemporary animation in reclaiming the older pioneering grammar of moving image practice enables the viewer to embrace the experience of 'seeing again' while 'seeing afresh'. In foregrounding technique alongside content, Dyer reveals Copenhagen in a completely different way than any travelogue or documentary could. Dyer's work bestrides cinema and gallery, time and technology, animation and animus, and effectively re-imagines animation through its long, lost past.

Dyer shoots his revolving cinetropes on a DV camera, creating a record of spinning loops and action cycles.

Chapter 03   Re-animating history   Reclaiming animation   112/113
              Re-defining practice   history II
              Re-thinking artists

Spinning cinetropes
suggest models of motion
in a gallery environment.

Dyer's cinetropes
simultaneously operate as
abstract forms and specific
types of documentary record,
both of the environment
itself and the process
of what might be termed
'archaic' technology.

RE-THINKING
ARTISTS

—

In an era of 'expanded cinema' or the
'manipulated moving image', animating
remains a traditional art in a progressive
context. Artists re-engage with history in
an attempt to liberate themselves from the
sometimes oppressive vocabularies of the
styles and contexts that inform dominant
practice. In the process, they have to rethink
their art through its formalist roots and
language. Where Dyer reclaimed the
language of pre-cinema, other artists
are revisiting the constituent tools of
expression in moving image forms to
express their vision.

Chapter 03   —
               Re-animating history
               Re-defining practice
               Re-thinking artists

—
114/115

**RE-TH
ARTIS**

—

—
—
—
—
—

KEYWORDS IN THIS SECTION

Installation
In recent years more and more animation
has found itself in gallery settings, often
informing and facilitating multimedia
installations of artefacts and moving image
artworks. This has provoked debates about
the status and definition of the work, as
there remains a resistance to naming these
aspects of moving image practice explicitly
as animation. Installation work often
affords the possibility of foregrounding
the procedural construction of animated
images and some of the material aspects
that inform it.

Cinematic apparatus
Within film study, the cinematic apparatus
has been understood as the viewing
principles, physical infrastructures and
delivery technologies, which facilitate
the execution of film exhibition and its
reception. This has necessarily had to take
into account the material aspects of creating
cinema, and the psychological, emotional and
physical experience of the viewer spectator.
With the digital shift, both the subject and
object of film study is under threat, and the
cinematic apparatus, though still extant is
necessarily re-thought and re-defined.

In an era of 'exp
'manipulated m
remains a tradit
context. Artists
an attempt to li
sometimes oppr
styles and conte
practice. In the
their art through
language. Where
language of pre-
are revisiting the
expression in mo
express their vis

03

ANIMATING LIGHT

—

Joost Rekveld's **#11, Marey <-> Moiré** project directly engages with the work of French scientist and pioneer chronophotographer, Étienne-Jules Marey. Rekveld explains: 'Film-maker Gerard Holthuis, who had some experience with producing semi-commercial films, wanted to try and break open the Dutch funding system for more experimental films. He liked my work and wondered what would happen if I were able to work on a bigger scale. We applied for the project and we actually managed to get a considerable grant. This enabled me to invest a lot of time in research and acquiring the technical skills I needed for making the film.

CHRONOPHOTOGRAPHY
—

#11, Marey <-> Moiré was informed by earlier films I had made. At the time, I was influenced by early abstract painters, such as Malevitch and Kandinsky and also by composers such as Stockhausen and Xenakis. In earlier films such as **#3** and **#5**, I used the principle of having a moving light source draw images during long exposures. In this way the movement of the light source generates both the images as well as the movement of those images by controlling the interference between the movement and the frame rate of the camera. Technically, **#11** was a next step by adding a shutter to this set-up. The images produced were the result of the interactions between the movement in front of the camera, the exposure time and the shutter frequency. At some point, I realised that the technique I was planning to use for **#11** was exactly what Marey did with his chronophotographs – cutting a long exposure

into bits by having a rotating shutter in front of the lens. I was already familiar with some of these pictures, but when I started to investigate more I was overawed by the inventiveness of the man. He invented many capturing devices and ways of taking pictures; he made mechanical models of organisms all of which are stunningly beautiful. His casual invention of the film camera and the film projector were completely beside the point for him; he was only interested in the science and the adequacy of his methods, which is probably why his results are so aesthetically pleasing as well.'

Rekveld is preoccupied by an intellectual interrogation of moving image practice, which engages with philosophical imperatives. 'I was reading the works of Henri Bergson, a French philosopher who wrote a lot about time and duration. At some point, he writes that only through art and intuition do we have access to the one, continuous evolution of the world, and that in the concept of our practical "mind time", it is necessarily discontinuous in order to get things done. In this context, for me, Marey represented this fundamental discontinuity in our methods to deal with anything practical. We can only solve a problem by chopping it into pieces and solving the bits. This is something fundamental to any technology. Marey represented the beauty of this principle and with my film I tried to remain as close to it as I could. Central to animation in my view is the notion of building up a complex world of movement out of tiny building blocks. This is both the technique and subject matter of **#11**. What I admire

Joost Rekveld works in his studio using the apparatus he constructed for his animated light project.

Chapter 03   Re-animating history   Animating light   116/117
             Re-defining practice
             Re-thinking artists

in all kinds of animation is how the world that is created is both completely artificial and very human, concepts that are often seen as incompatible. The craft of animation has to do with exactly this: how to "humanise" mechanical shapes by giving them motion qualities we can relate to.'

To make the film, Rekveld sought to disengage with the terms and conditions of contemporary apparatus and create a device that would enable him to record his aesthetic intentions. He notes: 'Before I built the machine I used to make **#11, Marey <-> Moiré**, I made a lot of sketches to help me imagine the kinds of images and movements it would generate. The idea was to make a film in-between the extremes given by the set-up I was using, for example, going from the minimum possible number of lines per frame to the maximum. Another pair of extremes concerned the location of the centre of rotation, going from as far away as was practically feasible to the centre of the frame. I used these extremes of all such parameters as the starting point of my composition.

'The second set of parameters were those of the optical printing process I used to combine the line patterns produced and add colour. I was using positive and negative versions of these patterns, and by combinations of bi-packing and superimposition, I could achieve many different kinds of layering. Some of these types of layering mimic what happens when objects pass in front of other objects, some simulate some kind of transparency and some are completely mathematical, dividing the screen into regions, the colour relations of which do not resemble the behaviour of familiar objects.'

Rekveld's use of formal parameters and his engagement with line forms are crucial, but his recognition of the temporal significance of layering – ironically, one of the key aspects in the reconfiguration of animation in the digital era – is equally important. Once more, an old-fashioned technique is revealed within the toolbox of contemporary work, one which effectively re-codes animation in a way that moves it beyond a frame-by-frame dynamic, into a deep frame-within-a-frame model.

Ultimately, this informs the conceptual interrogation of moving image practice, per se. Rekveld comments: 'In the end I am most interested by how our perception of the world is shaped by the concepts we have, concepts which can be verbal or non-verbal. The philosopher Nelson Goodman wrote that art does not imitate nature, but "nature is a product of art and discourse". I am interested in the history of science and in the history of art because I see them as the history of this discourse, the concepts of which are very often embodied in machines and methods of work. I came to film from a background in electronic music and computer composition.

'A big influence on my work was the Dutch composer and media theorist, Dick Raaijmakers, who I was lucky enough to have as one of my teachers. He has a special way of thinking about media by reducing them to their most basic model or set-up, and his way of thinking and the radicalism of his work were a big inspiration for me.

Rekveld is immersed in the mixture of traditional and new technologies required to facilitate an old technique for fresh aesthetic purposes. These redefine animation as the capture of moving light forms.

Three of the extraordinary
abstract images created
by Rekveld that play out
tensions between lines,
light forms and
colour transitions.

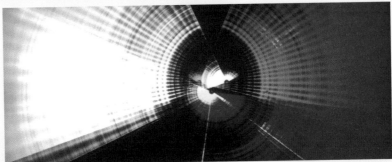

Chapter 03   Re-animating history   Animating light   118/119
               Re-defining practice
               Re-thinking artists

'When I became interested in experimental film the biggest discoveries for me were the films of James Whitney.
The **Five Abstract Film Exercises** he made, together with John Whitney, were very close to the kind of thinking about composition I was familiar with in contemporary music. His films **Yantra** and **Lapis** are astonishing works: I show them whenever I can and after seeing them hundreds of times, they still amaze me.'

EXPERIMENTAL TRADITION
—

Through working out of this experimental tradition, Rekveld readily sees that by re-engaging with technologies and established grammars of expression, there are always provocative ideas that can be readdressed through new technologies and grammars of expression, which can then emerge from cross-disciplinary practices.

'The developments I'm most interested in are those that seem to go toward systems in which images can somehow be "active". A lot of this work manifests itself in the current generation of laptop artists who often develop their own software to be able to "perform" their computer animations in real time. Artists such as Golan Levin also make image generators for others to interact with, either members of the public or other kinds of performers such as musicians or voice artists.

'The most interesting thing, I find, is the idea that in these systems, certain principles are embodied that can generate certain kinds of images, perhaps in interaction with other such systems. The most extreme example of where this might go is perhaps the International Society of Artificial Life community, where scientists are making very articulate computer models of living organisms or ecological systems, and where the idea is that one day there might be no reason anymore to not say that these simulations are themselves forms of life. I'm very much interested in these ideas and their possible application to art.'

Animation, in its most primal definition, means 'to breath life into', and in this progressive ambition is to become, then, the embodied essence of life itself.

According to Nelson Goodman 'nature is a product of art and discourse'. I am interested in the history of science and in the history of art because I see them as the history of this discourse, the concepts of which are very often embodied in machines and methods of work.
Joost Rekveld

ANIMATING SOUND

—

Rekveld's approach looks back at the way in which the cinematic apparatus itself could be understood as a generator of light and, consequently, of self-consciously constructed motion forms – the very stuff of animation. An often neglected aspect of the animation vocabulary, and an equally important tool, is sound. Carl Stalling and Scott Bradley defined the fragmentary soundtrack of the popular American animated cartoon, employing phrases and sequences from a variety of musical and sound idioms; Matyas Seiber and Francis Chagrin at the Halas & Batchelor Studio in England were two composers who extended the nature of the musical score for cartoons; while Pixar Animation think very carefully about the use of dialogue and sound effects in their stories. Every animator must think about the nature of sound in relation to the timing of the action.

THE ABSTRACT MATERIALS OF SOUND
—

Composer Brian Evans works in a more experimental tradition: '**Calidri** is one of a series of short animations that I think of as simple, visual music compositions. Music is the structuring of time using the abstract materials of sound. I am looking for ways to structure visual time in a musical way. I start with abstract visual materials and try to develop movements through visual consonance and dissonance, which can map to concepts of harmonic motion in Western instrumental music.'

In many senses, the crucial relationship between animation and sound remains relatively unexplored, under-assessed, and in some ways, undervalued. This is at the heart of some of Evans's preoccupations: 'To understand how important the relationship between sound and image is, I recommend the silent works of Stan Brakhage. As a composer, the correlation of image and sound is one of the things I am most interested in. I think there are degrees of tension and resolution that can be explored in abstract music and animation – in the images, the sound and in the relationship between the two.

'My work is computational, I work with numerical models, which are visualised and sonicated. I use all the tools available for algorithmic composition and generative art. I create visual scores (I call them time slices) from my abstract animations, which I then map into sound. The sonic becomes a metaphor for the visual and vice versa. My pieces build on a century-old tradition of visual music. I start with keyframes and then render in-betweens, composite and colour. I then add sound, which may sometimes find itself composited back into a remapped layer of the animation. It's an odd self-reflexivity. Image becomes sound and sound becomes image. These days I find myself drawn to the idea of metaphor – mapping from one conceptual domain to another.'

Chapter 03   Re-animating history   Animating sound   120/121
Re-defining practice
Re-thinking artists

LISTEN WITH YOUR EYES

Like other artists in this discussion, Evans
points to the intrinsically metaphoric nature
of animation and the way it can embody the
kinds of relationship between past, present
and future, as suggested in the previous
examples. Through metaphors, we connect
what we experience to what we know. We
create knowledge by connecting the new
(the present) to what we know (the past),
and so maybe predict what happens next
(the future).

Evans adds: 'I make maps.
The maps loop in time and in the moment.
There is synchrony in the sensory horizontal
and the temporal vertical. Image and audio
derive from the same numeric source. Each
maps the other in the moment and through
time. It's visual music in a synaesthetic
counterpoint. Musical narrative developed
over centuries, moving the listener through
time with the Pythagorean struggle of
harmonic conflict, dissonance seeking
consonance. My little loops engage that
struggle at various levels. Colour shifts.
Composition flows. Image and sound agree,
complement, disagree and resolve.'

Even in trying to describe
such a process, though, Evans makes an
important recommendation: 'Perhaps it's
abstract expressionism, true to its digital
materials, founded in musical traditions and
modernist formalism. But it's loosened a bit.
It's meant to be fun. It's jazz in colour,
shape, sound and computation. Relax.
Hear the colours. Listen with your eyes.'

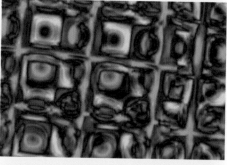

Evans's musical transitions
accompany the various
abstract metamorphoses of
shape, colour and form in
an ever-evolving image shift.

ANIMATING SPACE

—

Although sound and image constitute animation's core language, it has increasingly sought another dimension in its presence through space. Rose Bond, an experienced scholar and practitioner, has been eager to explore this sense of space, rejecting the gallery and preferring urban contexts to deliver her images. **Intra Muros** was one of the animated installations at the inaugural Platform Animation Festival in Portland in 2007. It took the extended platform for animation in all its forms as its key theme.

ENVISIONING SPACE

Bond notes: '**Intra Muros** is a departure from my earlier, historic, site-based installation work. With an autobiographical slant and themes that explored the creative process, it is less tied to a specific space, and could be staged in another building. The idea for the piece came during a personally difficult time. My original concept was entitled **In Situ** and it dealt with frustrations, loss of control and the overuse of organisational compulsions as coping devices. The physical metaphors evolved as I was animating. I believe the final piece finds resonance with many creatives – the empty mailbox, the call that doesn't come, the inspiration that eludes you. In making this piece I was aware that it would premiere at the inaugural Platform Festival and its first animated installation competition. I wanted to make a piece that was accessible to the public yet held particular meaning for animators. The allusions to experimental animators – auteurs who cut an edge in their own time –

speak to the idea of creative ancestry. An acknowledgement that individual genius is a myth and that, consciously or unconsciously, we ride on a river of work that flows from the past.

'**Intra Muros** means "within the walls". Quite literally, the animation is rear-projected on multiple windows from within the walls. It is viewed from the street. This public aspect – the whole idea of a mobile public, stopping, starting, looking, talking, texting and capturing is important. For me, the work stands apart from the traditional movie house; the no-cell zones of the multiplex; the self-containment of home video; and being apart from the hushed white space of galleries. It seems like public spectacle with the twist that it is also intimate. The voyeuristic aspect is evident from the start – the door opening to reveal a backlit silhouette entering, the personal rituals, and the distinctive gestures all glimpsed in unshuttered windows.'

Bond has carefully noted the reception of the piece: 'I have noticed that people tend to view the work several times. The loop is eight minutes. Speculating on this phenomenon, I believe this difference in viewing may be brought about by the scale, but even more so by the breaking up of the conventional screen. Not only is the action stretched over a longer viewing surface, well beyond peripheral vision, it is also broken or obscured by the mullions and walls. The viewer assumes what is happening behind the walls – possibly makes predictions – yet is periodically surprised. Animation provides endless opportunities to envision space.

Rose Bond's initial site-specific installation featuring animated silhouettes in framing devices on buildings was entitled **Illuminations**, and sought to shed light metaphorically on the building and its inhabitants.

Chapter 03   —   Re-animating history   —   Animating space   —
                          Re-defining practice   122/123
                          Re-thinking artists

Intra Muros creates and collapses space and time – from the minimally furnished realism of the studio/apartment to the graphic abstractions lifted from frames of a hand-drawn film leader, which twist again with a bursting forth of abstract movement and a presumption of psychological space. Finally, the linear layout of the windows presents several opportunities for interpretation. It is reminiscent of a four-panel newspaper comic strip – only these panels are animated. Just as Scott McCloud posits the power of the comic as lying between the gutter, also this piece appears to use the "gutter" of the walls to encourage a viewer to suture meaning from what is missing.'

REFLEXIVE ANIMATION
—

Bond's engagement with animation history, prompted a particular aesthetic approach: 'Aesthetically, I was going for two looks. The first being the long, moody set-up, in a monochromatic and dimly lit studio space. Here, the figure is three shades of grey and drawn with iconic facial simplicity – two dots for eyes. I imagined the second shorter section to be a visual sampling that referenced the experimental film-makers Len Lye and Norman McLaren. Animators generally have a self-awareness of their process. The sheer labour-intensity of it has been the subject matter of a number of films – Karen Aqua's **Vis-à-Vis** and to some

extent Daniel Greaves's **Manipulation**. **Intra Muros** finds kinship with media/creative process-referenced works with its in-joke visual samplings – the chicken from McLaren's **Hen Hop** and the bands of dancing colour from Lye's **A Colour Box**.'

This notion of the self-reflexive and self-figurative in animation is present throughout the history of animation from its earliest forms, an insistent characteristic that Bond believes will underpin the nature of future work in the form: 'Animation as popular entertainment will continue to reap box office rewards and cable options. The change I see coming is this: digital tools are all too available to artists of every medium. In academia, the walls between the disciplines are dissolving. Art students are moving between platforms and the call of the sequenced image is compelling. I believe animation, or frame-by-frame thinking, will be increasingly prevalent in intermedia works that combine sculpture, performance and projection.

'I'm drawn to animation that lives outside the movie house; work that is consciously modulating the perception or experience of time to achieve its cognitive and emotive ends; work that implicates the viewer in a larger context; work that is thoughtfully articulated within a space – that articulation being essential to its experience.'

Bond's execution of the piece enabled the public to engage with experimental film practice in an accessible public space. It allowed the viewer to enjoy the aesthetic elements of the work for its own sake and become aware of the references to other animation artists including Norman McLaren and Len Lye.

N
NED

'OBJECT REACT'

—

—
04

'OB
—
0

RE-ANIMATING
PEDAGOGY

—

As previously suggested throughout this discussion, there are significant issues in relation to the ways in which animation may be taught. A range of viewpoints has been implicitly and explicitly offered, which effectively note three core models.

First, a quasi-training model, dedicated to preparing practitioners to be members of collaborative teams, using industry-level software and technique on major studio projects. Second, a more auteurist, independent model, encouraging the creation of individual works, which signal the intention to be an autonomous artist. Third, an often uneasy combined model, offering a comprehensive education in which knowledge and skills are developed through individual and collaborative projects, which engage with a variety of theoretical and practice idioms, and which encourage participants to find their own level and outlook. Some educators prioritise the technical process, while others emphasise the significance of 'the idea'. Some make claims for the value of generic and transferable skills, others, more highly specific abilities. Ultimately, the ones being educated need to have innate talent and vision.

The next section presents a project undertaken by Johnny Hardstaff and Darryl Clifton, in collaboration with the Victoria & Albert Museum, Onedotzero, the Institute of Contemporary Arts and Loughborough University – **Object React**. A number of established student practitioners were invited to partake in the project. The project was predicated upon developing a moving image response to an artefact from the Victoria & Albert Museum. It interrogated the process by which creative practice in animation might be in some way 'taught', and what particularly underpinned this approach.

RE-AN
PEDA

—

KEYWORDS IN THIS SECTION

Education
Animation is an intrinsically metaphorical,
and sometimes metaphysical, language of
expression. Further, it is a direct and
accessible form even when using simple iconic
images to express complex ideas. It has
always been used in educational contexts as
an important aid to teaching and learning.
Crucially, in the contemporary era, the
personal statements and approaches in
animation, especially when grounded in
core historical knowledge and experience,
all serve to educate in different ways,
reflecting the convergence, divergence
and challenges of different disciplines
and cultural outlooks.

Pedagogy
Methods and approaches to teaching a
discipline that must be modified as
disciplines change and develop, or
tailored in accordance with different
methods of delivery.

As previously su
discussion, there
relation to the w
be taught. A rang
implicitly and ex
effectively note t

dedicated to prep
members of colla
industry-level so
major studio proj
auteurist, indepe
the creation of in
the intention to b
Third, an often un
offering a compre
knowledge and sk
individual and col
engage with a var
practice idioms, a
participants to fir
outlook. Some ed
technical process

SETTING
THE BRIEF

—

Brief

Contemporary media is engaged in an incessant search for 'the new', 'the modern' and 'the progressive'.

Rarely does one hear the words 'antiquity', 'heritage' and 'museum' used in reference to the inspiration and cultivation of new, original and progressive work.

This is somewhat ironic, considering that there can be few paths to deeply original and exciting work as direct as the simple merging of one's own rich heritage, with contemporary thought and the medium of new technologies.

Produce a communicative visual response to one of the artefacts/exhibits that has been curated specifically for this project. Research your chosen exhibit. Understand its history, its original purpose and the nature of its manufacture. Unearth its tears, its blood and emotional state. Unearth both its past and its future potential, and communicate your evaluation in a revelatory and communicative manner that goes far beyond not just the accepted and familiar language of museums, but that also directly challenges the contemporary expectations/dialogues/ aesthetics of contemporary work.

The careful selection of these exhibits has ensured that each has its own story and that each has had its own impact.

Many of these exhibits have a great cultural significance. Many have been deeply fetishised at some point in their existence. There are both examples of monastic craft and of mass production. Several of these exhibits are the sole survivors of their craft, but overall, all are in some way mute.

Poignantly, we are asking you to play 'Dorian Gray' with these objects. Discover your exhibit's true representation. We know what it physically looks like within its display case, but what does it really represent? What is its true image? Is a coveted treasure in some sense conceited, all too aware of its value? Is a religious, devotional icon theologically pure, or perhaps pious and political? Are the spoils of war unaffected by the human horrors committed in their acquisition?

What of your chosen object's current environment? We understand the function of museum collections... don't we? Why do we value antiquity? Indeed, why has your object been selected (and above so many others) for public exhibition at all, and what does that say about us? What do we project upon these exhibits? What is it that we want from these cultural artefacts and what can they deliver from within their glass exhibition cases?

Discover your exhibit's resonance, both literally and metaphorically. Ultimately, find its frequency and make it speak again.

Chapter 04   Re-animating pedagogy   Setting the brief   128/129
             Process   The student/mentor exchange
             Practice

THE STUDENT/
MENTOR EXCHANGE

The following set of extracts and images feature the work of stop-motion animator and animation archivist, Kerry Drumm. Her statements are retrospective accounts of her experience; the comments from Johnny Hardstaff and Darryl Clifton were made as the project was progressing. The 'teaching points' are those drawn out of the responses as ways of thinking about teaching and learning within creative, moving image practice. This is a particularly interesting case, as the project saw Drumm move from her discipline as an animator to that of a live-action director.

Drumm: When we were first handed the brief for the **Object React** project, I was initially drawn to the fashion section. It's always been the first place I visit when I walk into the V&A, and mainly the costumes. I took photos of the dress and crinoline chosen for the project and bought a book to research the artefact. I was first interested in the crinoline, which is a framed petticoat worn under the dress to create the fullness of the skirt. I then began thinking about the secrecy of the crinoline, hidden under the mass of fabric. The idea of 'privacy' and women getting dressed and undressed behind screens were some of the first images I considered. I began thinking of Simon Pummell's film **The Secret Joy of Fallen Angels** and how Simon filmed behind a screen. I was also preparing myself to make the film as a stop-motion animation film.

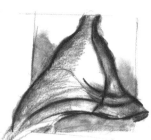

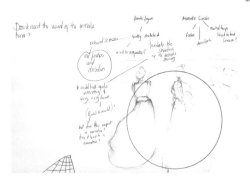

Drumm's initial sketches for her film, **Beneath**, consider the technical, aesthetic and conceptual elements of the piece.

Two of Drumm's mood boards set the tone, atmosphere and culture of her approach to the aesthetic premise of the piece.

Teaching Points

—

The creative and provocative nature of the brief in itself should be inspiring and challenging. It should immediately incite an investment in the work and prompt an immediate engagement with relevant research, the development of conceptual ideas and an affiliation with other works that might enable, influence, or provide pertinent stimulus.

—

—

—

Drumm: It was important for me to try and explain or represent the freedom that the crinoline petticoat gave to the women of that period. Previously, to create the fullness of the dress, women wore many layers of petticoats. The fashion was a corseted waist and a very full dress. The results were often women fainting due to the heat caused by the layers of material. What the crinoline offered was the removal of the petticoats and the wearing of one frame. In today's society I imagine many would view the crinoline as a cage, almost representing kept creatures, but the thing I was keen to express was that the invention of the crinoline was a vast improvement in women's fashion!

Teaching Points

—

Resonant art normally grows out of an engagement with the historical, political and social parameters that inform the context in which the work is made.

—

Finding a level of personal empathy with the ideas and concepts formed underpins highly motivated work and results in the desire to say something through aesthetic practice. This does not necessarily have to be an overtly political statement, but should be about the formal engagement of what the work is about, what it is for, and who it is for.

—

—

—

Drumm: With the crinoline, I wanted to represent the idea of lightness, but I also wanted to represent the weight women experienced when wearing the many layers of petticoats. This kept me awake at night. Then I thought of water and how fabric becomes heavy when soaked with water. All sorts of ideas crept into my head – 'I know, let's have a woman in a full skirt walk into sea and film it'. Not a bad idea, but how could I film it?

A friend of mine who works for the RSPCA mentioned a dog hydrotherapy pool, which seemed ideal. The owner was happy to help. I explained what I wanted to do with the water – film my friend in the dress to represent heaviness. Then for the second part, still film stop-motion the frames behind a screen, but removing the secrecy – I wanted to try and let the crinoline frames dance, almost in a waltz-like state.

Teaching Points

Invention should always be allied with pragmatism and often the best practice comes out of the most creative use of limited resources. In many educational contexts it often has to!

If an idea has some resonance and quality, there is almost always a way in which it can be 'tested' in its execution. Thinking ahead in pre-production can save time, energy and resources.

Hardstaff/Clifton: Fantastic. What a great call, shooting it underwater. In doing so you both convey the original sense of liberation that you feel the cage to have brought women, but still emphasise the female bondage side of things through the weight of sodden layers of fabric in water that you quite rightly identify as tangible.

Three technical points for you: when shooting fabric in water, you will find that whilst the fabric moves slowly, you still might want to be able to shoot at a higher frame rate (around 50 frames per second) and have the option of frame cutting later. The balletic quality you will be able to get from it we think you will ultimately find very seductive, so you may wish to plan ahead on this. The technical staff has a three-chip camera that shoots in an approximation of frames, rather than fields and it shoots at different frame rates. We believe it will also record wonderfully at low light (underwater).

Secondly, yes, you can buy (or hire) transparent bags and cases for taking cameras underwater, certainly for the kind of depths you're talking about. They're inexpensive and effective. The camera isn't an issue, the operation of the camera is. If you want this to be hand-held (and the wonder of water is that it gives you a natural and cheap steadicam) then you're fine. But you might well want your shots to be locked off, and if so, you need to get hold of a tripod or build some kind of simple brace mechanism so that the camera stays in its bag and is fine. Actually, we think some of these bags have tripod mounts.

Thirdly, how you light this is an issue. We would overcompensate with lighting sources and have as much as you can in terms of variety and nature. Why not look into doing some experiments with a stills camera, the bath and odd lighting choices (UV, for example)? It really depends what you want to convey. Do you need to get lights underwater? If so, and we can see why this would be good, look at custom underwater lights.

Lastly, think carefully about the pool that you select to shoot in. What colour is the pool, not just on camera but also behind camera? If it is not what you desire, either find another pool or just find the appropriate tonal qualities in plastic sheeting and dress it.

Also, and this is just for our own conscience if nothing else, please remember that this might be very dangerous.

In today's society, I imagine many would view the crinoline as a cage, almost representing kept creatures, but the thing I was keen to express was that the invention of the crinoline was a vast improvement in women's fashion!
Kerry Drumm

Teaching Points

Teaching Points

–

Once a core concept or idea has been accepted and work gone into its potential execution, it is crucial that technical matters are addressed, not merely in relation to the management of equipment itself, but also to the pertinence of its use for aesthetic and conceptual outcomes.

–

Technical knowledge is important and in some senses objective, but it should also be used in a subjective sense in order to suggest ideas to the practitioner. In this sense, the student/mentor bond is collaborative at one level, as the more experienced mentor must offer perspectives that will enable the best outcome for the work, which the practitioner may not have considered.

–

Health and safety is absolutely paramount in securing professionally engaging outcomes. Health and safety advice normally helps in the organisational and procedural aspects of developing work effectively in all creative environments.

–

–

–

Drumm: It was put to me at the brief that I shoot the whole film underwater. But what about animating? I animate! At first I wouldn't even think about it – but then on the train home I began to think how it could be done. I have no idea how I came to the idea, except through a conversation about a large fish tank being for sale, which also kept me awake for a number of nights!

–

Sometimes a practitioner needs and requires radical challenge; on some occasions, practical advice and on others, comfort, consolation and support. Remaining sensitive to the artistic, conceptual and practical needs of a piece of work should prompt empathic and accurate mentor support.

–

–

–

Hardstaff/Clifton: We're very sorry to hear that what we had suggested has in any way thrown you, if indeed it has.

The last thing we want to do is confuse you or in any way deflate or unnerve you. Please excuse us if we are a little direct. We just find it more expedient.

However, the apologies do need to end there, because we do want to constructively test your ideas, and we do want to help you question what it is you are doing, and how you are doing it.

It strikes us very strongly that your underwater filming is the strongest aspect of your proposed film. You must be careful in throwing different media together in the subsequent sections. You're going to undo all the good work with unrelated sequences that follow.

It is vital that at every juncture when making films, you test, question and sound out your plans and ideas.

All we fear is that you are overcomplicating things and therefore will dilute what it is you are saying.

Privately, you may know you're right. That's the nature of film-making. Sometimes you just have to do it, and then see what your audience feels. The only way to learn is to risk making both good and bad mistakes.
Johnny Hardstaff

Chapter 04

Re-animating pedagogy
Process
Practice

The student/mentor exchange

132/133

Teaching Points

We think this is nothing to have a sleepless night over. It is effortlessly redeemable by simply dropping the unnecessary.

It is also very important that, as a director, you follow your vision, and at times, be very bloody minded about it. You live and die by what it is you make. If you know better, then follow your gut instinct. After all, this is about your voice. However, if any of this raises doubts, then you may want to listen to these doubts, as they may well have some weight.

We think that directing requires strength of vision more than anything else. Privately, you may know you're right. That's the nature of film-making. Sometimes you just have to do it and then see what your audience feels. The only way to learn is to risk making both good and bad mistakes.

Once again, the testing process never stops until the edit is over. But you should really be sleeping more soundly after a discussion like that, because it may well have stopped you making a mistake, or made you more confident of your ideas and how individualistic and visionary your approach is.

—

Couched in the right terms, the mentor can always be a provocateur, enabling the practitioner to test assumptions and evolving ideas, being a sounding board, devil's advocate and critical friend. The only object is to help the practitioner secure the best outcome for the work, and this means that the practitioner must engage carefully with their own decision-making process in order to be absolutely secure about attaining their desired goal.

—

Seeking the right balance of material in a moving-image piece is important. There is often the tendency to do too much or include material that is not absolutely required. Knowing what to edit and excise is as much of a key skill as knowing what to include.

—

Finding stimuli, whether admired or despised, is helpful in continuing to discover the motives and imperatives of the work as it proceeds, and encourages, clear decision-making.

—

Taking risks, making mistakes and learning from experience is an absolute requirement for any developmental creative process.

Drumm: At this point I had included a few folk to help make the film. Talented composers, Jode Steel and David Wainwright from Verbal Vigilante Music, were brought in for the soundtrack. It was really important to have the music mirror what I was trying to say. We met a number of times to discuss my ideas and the brief I had been given. They were excited about the film being shot underwater as it gave them a strong artistic direction to follow and enabled them to set some of their own parameters regarding the instrumentation and feel of the piece. Cellos and basses were used to mirror the movement of the dress underwater. Dynamic swells were used to highlight the unusual and restricted flow. My friend Aaron Wood was also keen to edit the film – he was learning After Effects and wanted to put the training into practice.

      I discovered that the dog hydrotherapy pool had an underwater camera so we all headed to the Wirral for a day's shooting. My friend, Katie Steed, agreed to model the old bridesmaid's dress. I purchased shoes and a jacket and my mum made bloomers. I was so nervous. I had no idea how this was going to look – we were shooting blind. The underwater camera at the pool wasn't high quality and frustratingly the dress kept changing colour. I had purchased an underwater camera bag that would fit my family's DV camera, but I didn't quite trust it. However, we kept shooting and had over an hour of material; the majority of the best clips were when Katie was trying to flatten the dress ready for a shot, so quite accidental.

      The next part was to shoot the crinolines in the fish tank. I spent a couple of weeks making the crinolines. I suppose my years of making puppets and sets contributed to my being able to do this. I had been able to source a camera arm from Loughborough, which enabled me to attach my DV camera to a chair. The plan was for the chair to move slowly along the tank while the crinolines swayed back and forth creating a free-floating feeling. This worked really well, and I was happy with how it looked.

      When it came to editing, we had problems with the dress changing colour in the hydrotherapy pool and there were clips that we simply could not use and this was frustrating. We had no control as to how everything moved while filming in water. This was so different to what I was used to. With animation, you know exactly where A to B is and you have a storyboard to follow. With the footage I had, it was so frustrating trying to link clips and create a sequence.

These images show the complexities of shooting the dress underwater.

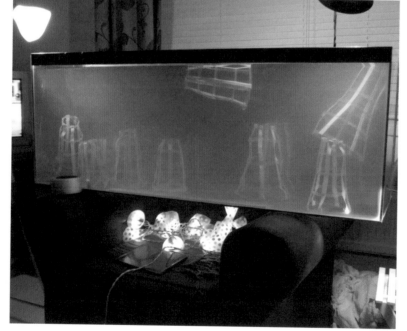

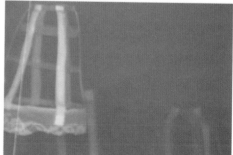

The above images show
the fish tank where the
crinolines were floated
and shot. Practical and
domestic sacrifices
are often part of the
creative process.

Hardstaff/Clifton: So, we have seen it. Really interesting. Part 1 has lovely movements and qualities, and Part 2 is truly quite beautiful and magical, ethereal even. Together they are enigmatic and quietly provocative. Great stuff.

There are, however, a few things holding the film back from being much better still. Darryl and I have sat down together and watched your film many times, and the following points, if addressed, we feel would improve things greatly.

Ideally, we would like you to think about this, and if possible, address them. Of course, this is your call, and these are just our opinions:

Part 1

01: Is there an odd filter/blur/high-contrast effect applied to it? If so, we would be very tempted to remove it. The neat footage would look very nice just that, 'neat'.

02: The background that you have inserted, we personally think, is not so convincing. The hue is almost OK, so perhaps all it needs is a lovely pale or duck egg blue colour of some kind, rather than the textured version you have inserted. There seems to be a conflict of texture. Maybe let the fabric speak for itself without this visual confusion between the back- and foreground.

03: The pace of the edit is very much off. Frankly, this is a very poor edit indeed. The first cut is harsh, awkward and ill-timed. Then it jumps to dissolves. Where is the logic and rationale to this edit? Every edit must have a logical system that it adheres to. Also, the edit is out of time with the music. When the hand brushes down the fabric, the dramatic cello lunge happens a good second after.

04: Seeing the model's feet kills abstract, otherworldly sensations. It somewhat kills the illusion. The more screen that is filled with the billowing fabric, the better, perhaps?

Part 2

01: A touch too long. Also, 17 seconds of credits is utterly unnecessary. Our guideline on duration was only ever a suggestion. It is more about what the film needs.

02: Do you think titles and credits kill your film a little? We do. It is a very conventional way of saying here is a contrived cinematic experience. They are unnecessary. Does the whole world need to know who edited it for instance? On such a short film, it is very heavy-handed. The solitary word 'Beneath' would surely suffice. All these names and credits scream two words: 'artifice' and 'mundane'.

03: The type/calligraphy is historically inaccurate and a little twee. It does not feel like convincing script, let alone script of the period; there is way too much text. Somehow, it cheapens the film and makes it feel a little amateur. As do the immortal words 'A film by...'.

We are only writing this because we would very much like to see this film included in the showcase. The second part is gorgeous. If you act on this, we genuinely believe this will help the film enormously and guarantee exhibition at the ICA, inclusion on the Onedotzero touring programme, and the V&A Web profile.

The shot captures the weight and lyricism of the floating dress.

Teaching Points

It is important to identify the strengths of any one piece first, before its shortfalls and suggestions for improvement are identified.

Criticism can come in many forms, but must always be depersonalised and constructive. Evaluating creative work problematises this process because matters of taste can undermine a more objective position. Alternative points of view about aesthetics can only be offered in a spirit of 'please consider this as a possible improvement to your work'.

At times, there are occasions that require an emphatic point due to clear inadequacies that undermine the material. The work must always be judged on its best terms and conditions, and at least given the opportunity for the fairest, and hopefully, most positive evaluation.

Crucial to all production processes is the best use of time in the facilitation of key goals. The pre-production process is absolutely fundamental in determining how a schedule should be created, managed, and adhered to.

Best advice should encourage practitioners to avoid cliché and to make sure that all the elements of the work result in a coherent statement and outcome. Best practice should recognise the importance of the process in achieving planned and notable ends.

Drumm: If I remove the colour correction and the filters the film will revert to the red of the dress. I was afraid to use this as I wasn't sure if it would work with the second part of the film. I would have to remove the opening section of the moving hand across the dress – this was filmed quite brown as the camera was refocusing at the time and it was an accidental shot. Unless I can change the colour of the dress, of course. I love the idea of duck egg, but not sure this will work if I revert to red. What do you think?

I have just spoken to the guys who did the music. The music for the first part was already composed, and they composed to the footage I had in Part Two. We all think it's better if I re-edit the first bit and the composition for it.

Credits are gone! Do I need to put my name at the end of the film? I suppose I was not confident enough to trust my instincts with the footage. I wanted to slow down the dress more, but was afraid of not using enough of the other shots. Do you think this will work, slowing some of the dress movement?

Teaching Points

—

It is important to sustain an open and honest dialogue throughout the course of a project and consider questions and ideas right until completion.

—

Encouraging personal appraisal is crucial, particularly in identifying the strengths of a project, as well as its possible shortfalls.

—

Enabling practitioners to consider their recommendations for improvement on the next occasion is one of the most significant parts of the process.

—

—

Drumm: I am happy with the end result of the film. It took a couple of goes editing the film, and the soundtrack is stunning. And as always, I wish I could make the film again. As for making the film all live action – I quite enjoyed it. It was different to anything I had done before.

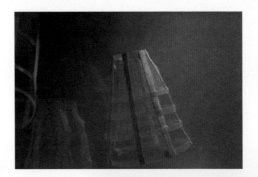

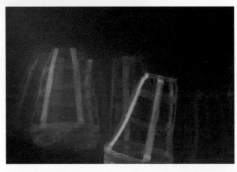

The crinolines float away sublimely in the water, symbolising the ways in which women were liberated from the very weight of their garments; it also reflects their rapidly changing identity.

PROCESS

—

It is sometimes useful to think of a project purely in terms of its intellectual challenge and the ways in which its core themes are discussed and developed. This can sometimes be contentious within an arts context, directly pitting form and aesthetics against social and cultural inference, and placing the political dimension of the work into clear relief.

Process, for all its material concerns, needs to be understood as a model of learning that moves from an initial conception into a period of research and development. This adds and consolidates ideas. Consequently, the work will start to gain conceptual focus and thematic clarity. It is crucial to maintain this intellectual understanding as the work is executed. Remaining conscious about what can be achieved during its execution moves the work beyond technical application, and maximises the creative potential accordingly.

PROC

—

KEYWORDS IN THIS SECTION

Visualisation

Traditional scripts for film and television
are predicated on the construction of
narrative through descriptors and dialogue.
They must necessarily embrace story, plot,
style, genre, etc. This approach may also
be pertinent to making animated films and
television programmes, but it is more
often the case that animation is developed
through processes of visualisation. This
includes development sketches, model
sheets, storyboarding and layout material.
It could also take on an informal and
improvised guise, depending on the
materials and techniques chosen.

Re-historicisation

In an era that is preoccupied with the
present, a process of 're-historicisation'
is increasingly important. This is
essentially a re-engagement with history
to prevent the past becoming a set of
heritage-based stereotypes and soundbite
conclusions. Re-historicisation also seeks
to reclaim lost and marginalised aspects
of the past.

It is sometimes
project purely in
challenge and th
themes are disc
can sometimes
context, directly
against social ar
placing the polit
into clear relief.

concerns, needs
of learning that
conception into a
development. Th
ideas. Consequen
gain conceptual
It is crucial to m
understanding as
Remaining consc
achieved during
work beyond tec
maximises the cr

CHOICE, CHANGE
AND CHALLENGE

—

Lydia Hawkins embraced the **Object React** project through exemplary research and exercised considerable thought in relation to her political and aesthetic position in interpreting her chosen object. This resulted in an extended and complex debate with the tutors – Hardstaff and Clifton – which offers an interesting example of the 'call and response' that can heighten and problematise artistic practice.

FEBRUARY 24TH 2006
—

Hawkins: I am pretty much decided now that I plan to do something with the Wedgwood Cameo, so if she could put me in touch with someone from that department that would be great.

    Hardstaff/Clifton: Good luck. Think about contacting Wedgwood directly. You can probably get information that not only talks about the historical-contextual implications of the object, but also its manner of production, relative cost, and who it was sold to, for example.

MARCH 6TH 2006
—

Hawkins: I have spoken to the Wedgwood museum and unfortunately they do not have records from this period; the person I spoke to was unable to give further information about who it was distributed to, etc. However, I know from previous research that it is estimated up to 15,000 were made (but this is only an estimate) and they were distributed to supporters to wear. Wedgwood bore the cost of these, and again, it is estimated that they sold for three pounds and three shillings each – a selling price of approximately £198 in today's

currency. The contact was able to tell me a bit more about the production, which is white jasper with a black jasper relief. Wedgwood came up with the right formulae for jasper after thousands of experiments to get it just right, which he did only a few years before the slave medallion was created. Obviously this would have been a very exciting and productive time for him and his involvement in the abolition society would mark a huge point of change in lots of ways. All his other correspondence show his commitment to the cause.

    In the society in which he was operating, he would have had to mix in higher class circles to advance his business; it seems pretty likely these individuals would have been wearing the medallions in a similar way that Bono and Madonna support charities today.

    I am now going to continue researching into some visual ideas that have come out of this research.

MARCH 7TH 2006
—

Hardstaff/Clifton: Thank you for sending your document/treatment over.

    Please excuse us if this email is in any way provocative or confrontational. We think that is our job on this project: to prompt.

    As you know, we are, of course, very excited about the specific object that you have chosen, as we discussed.

    We understand the parallel that you have chosen with the modern day and the trade in white female sex slaves. Absolutely, this seems a most natural parallel to draw.

In the face of considerable challenge to the conceptual interpretation of her chosen object, Lydia Hawkins used her research and her own preoccupations to determine her work. The dialogue shows the complexity of creating work, and serves as a critical discourse on the issues, which can be addressed as a consequence of resonant moving-image practice.

Written treatment for
onedotzero/V&A
Object React project
—

Object: Wedgwood Cameo for the Abolition of the Slave Trade, 1787
—

—

—

—

A tiny, delicate, relatively expensive item to produce, highly crafted and using the latest technologies of the day, the cameo's appearance in terms of material is deceptive. As the words on the cameo say, the piece is actually shouting about the horrors it represents. I have researched how much impact it really had and whether a black person would have ever seen these cameos. Who wore them? It would have been 'high' society members of the day (and it probably would have been very fashionable in certain circles to wear one), in a similar way to stars wearing white bands now in terms of making a current statement, although the design of the compared items is hugely different. It appears the cameos did have an impact and as they were made when the Society for the Abolition for the Slave Trade was founded in 1787, marked a great time of change and a real chance for the Slave Trade to stop.

The visual language of that time is equally as deceptive in terms of its seduction; the ornate handwriting that logged the names and details of the slaves, the items acquired that were a direct result of either profit from the trade or goods used for products from the trade, like a silver sugar vase, and the lavish excess of the wealth that was created from the slave trade shown in fabrics and ceramics from the time, which marked the start of the export and import trade.

The language of the image of the slave on the cameo, his pose, kneeling down pleading is European of that time in its depiction of a black person, similar to other illustrations of the period, slightly caricatured and generic. Wedgwood wrote that it would gain people's pity and as a means to an end to try to gain support from people who would understand this language it worked.

After researching the actual object and Wedgwood's involvement in the movement, and possible suggestions that Wedgwood's motivation for creating it were in part to gain credibility and help his business - though through research this seems unlikely now - I have broadened my area for what's to be included in the sequence. There is some speculation that Wedgwood's prior business was with people who quite possibly could have been slave traders; in 1775 he accepted a commission to make a 'nest of baths' for an African King (please see Mary Guyatt's essay **The Wedgwood Slave Medallion, Values in Eighteenth-century design**).

I liked the very graphic feel of the cameo, starkly black on white. Along with my research into the Atlantic slave trade in the 17th and 18th century, I looked at the current slave trade, which includes sex trafficking of white woman all over the world. Also Sierra Leone kept coming up in my research, which was once a former British colony. In the same year the cameo was created, a settlement for freed slaves was established, which was then attacked by one of the neighbouring chiefs in 1789. Thomas Clarkson wrote to Wedgwood about this.

Today children work as slaves in the diamond mines near Koidu Town, the capital of the Kono district of the Republic of Sierra Leone. The visual language of the diamond and sex trade is also seductive in the same way as the material wealth created from the slave trade. It has even been argued that members of popular culture actually fuel and glamorise the sex trade.

The international trafficking of women for the sex trade is one of the slave trades that still exists now, which includes women and girls of all races. I will contrast the image of the black man with that of a white woman today. And will quote both the original printed phrase on the cameo: 'Am I not a man and a brother?' and the contemporary version 'Am I not a woman and a sister?'. I will draw on the elements of human greed, the slave trade then and now, Sierra Leone and the thread between them being the diamonds, which are perceived as displaying wealth, money and power, an indication of human greed then and now, which is also what the sex trafficking is for, to satisfy a greed.

The sequence will start with the cameo and tell the story of how it came to be made, a little about what came before and compare it with the sex slave trade now, contrasting graphically between white and black, possibly with silhouetted figures using a very limited palette of black, white and silver. Ending with a new 'cameo' design inverted of a white woman, perhaps amongst some calling cards, echoing the mass-produced black-and-white pamphlets/photocopies that would have been produced for the abolition movement in the 1780s.

However, in brief, we need to ask you this: Is slavery over for the black race?

In our minds it is not over at all. If you look at the USA, not to mention the UK or any underpaid service industry, and you will see that its employment (by modern, rich, white industrial masters) is very heavily black. This is, in the West, a near universal story. Black prospects are economically limited; racism is rife; this is endless.

Why get away from the point of the object, if the point, made over 200 years ago, is still an issue? Why is the professional side to the City of London almost exclusively white, but the restaurant workers, cleaners, traffic wardens almost universally black? Is lowly paid employment not slavery? On the plantations slaves were fed. Then is that not payment?

We are not trying to make this complicated for you and we are not trying to upset your plans. We think that everything you have done so far could be applied to many causes, but this is about your object. This object has an incredible purpose and overall, has been ineffective. Can you not further its cause? Can you not begin to redress this imbalance? Can you not find the modern comparison in black/white race relations today?

We think you are ducking the issue in some ways. You are dealing with monochromatic imagery, in this instance, black and white. It is literal for a purpose. There is a glorious single-mindedness about Wedgwood.

What do you think? Where do you stand on the treatment of black people in modern society or the separatism that exists?

MARCH 9TH 2006

—

Hawkins: When I initially researched the object, I was taken aback by it and then thought it was about hope, then I came across all the information about Wedgwood's involvement and motivations, which I mention in the treatment. Of course, abolition did not achieve equality and so I looked at the actual 'slave' trades that still exist, but are hardly discussed in the media or day to day. I was approaching it from this angle, and almost using the ideas within the cameo to address what that means today.

This issue of poverty and slavery, as you say, is huge, global and still very much alive all over the world. Extreme poverty and starvation as a result of a debt, corrupt governments and not being able to trade are just some of the reasons the problems continue. This still happens while people enjoy extreme wealth and carry small dogs in designer bags with diamond-encrusted dog collars on the other side of the world.

For my presentation I was aiming to interpret a current-day take on a literal interpretation of slavery today – that although the 'slaves' have changed in terms of what they do, it's still a universal problem. However, I welcome your comments about this project and will look further into it in these terms.

Other issues I was aware of/related to my ideas on the object:

—
1. Other inequalities in this country including class.

—
2. Inequality in race in Europe and areas in the Middle East and Asia.

—
3. Inequality within one race in countries like India where there is a caste system.

I do take your comments on board, but as there is only a limited timescale on this project, I have to have a cut-off point to my research.

There are many ways the object can be interpreted: from the period it was created and what was happening then; the inequalities between races then – specifically slavery; and what that object means now in this country, the West and the USA. I was interested in what the object's future might be and I was focusing on inequalities directly linked to modern day slavery in the most literal way.

The written treatment was my idea for the project and not by any means set in stone. I feel that this object opens up many questions rather than answering any, and therefore would aim to do this with my piece, looking at the issues I've mentioned previously.

MARCH 11TH 2006
—

Hardstaff: Thank you for writing. Ultimately, I do feel you should stick to your guns, and do it your way. However, my last thought for you is this:

Having worked outside of the white middle class enclave that is education, let alone the ultra liberalism that is 'art school', and having worked at Billingsgate fish market, New Covent Garden market, hospitals and mortuaries, and having travelled widely and having mixed race children, I would say that the vast majority of this country are card carryingly racist to their core. 'Does still go on?' is an enormous understatement. It is the absolute norm – the problem is still there. You must do what it is you want to do, but personally (and this should have no bearing on what you do) I really do feel you are completely ducking the issue. The issue is there in black and white for you.

Hawkins: I am very grateful for your input on this. I may be wrong but the reason I went down the point of view I did previously was because I felt that the following points were significant to the object and the project I had researched, and I wanted to take a wider view on the topic and to show it is happening (modern day slavery) in areas that people may not assume straight away.

I did not and do not feel I was intentionally ducking issues to do with the object, but decided to take this point of view. I had not finalised my storyboard as I was still in contact with you over the project.

CRITICAL
EXAMPLES

—

The following imagery is drawn from two projects undertaken in the **Object React** initiative, each one a particular address of the practice of visualisation and the re-imagining of animation on personal terms and conditions. Both focus on developing a core concept their aesthetic practice seeks to illustrate, and each uses the dynamic palette of the animated form to reinvent physical environments, and promote different ways of seeing.

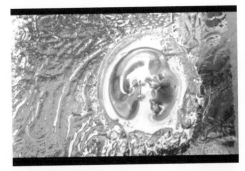

The fluidity of changing subjective material, physical and emotional states is caught in the metamorphoses of distortion and malleability in the objective environment.

girl waits for someone to come home...as she openes the door, she is transformed into a glassblown moment...

Kristina Hoffman's simple but highly evocative **Glassviews** takes as its starting point that 'life isn't about perfect moments, but about seeing the imperfections in a perfect way'. Influenced by the work of Carl Nordbruch, Hoffman seeks to find the perfection in imperfection by capturing moments of anticipation - the seconds before revelation and fulfilment. This is achieved through a lyrical series of distortions of everyday incidents as they might be seen through the curvature of blown glass.

The **Object React** initiative proved to be pivotal in enabling the re-historicisation of objects through developing aesthetic applications. By using animation as a tool to re-imagine these objects, their histories, their impact, and their symbolic and associative import, some important political and ideological principles were rediscovered. All these had pertinence to a contemporary world that insists upon the particular and specific focus of the present at the expense of what has gone before. The project enabled practitioners to theorise their approach through practice, and practice through their theoretically determined outlooks, each project recovering history as a model of progressive activity, both in the development of contemporary moving image practice and as a model of socio-cultural learning and advancement.

Ulrika Axen and Tobias Rudquist built a 3D tensegrity structure that they could interact with and animate upon. In a persuasive mix of 2D and 3D elements, the film plays with compositional conventions and a variety of performance idioms. The artist and the camera intervene with the implied visual dynamics of the frame. The film plays out a metaphor concerning the natural success of the living organism the tensegrity structure represents, and the failure of destructive man-made industrial structures and processes.

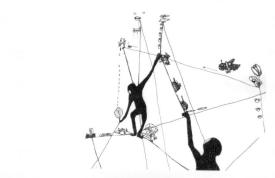

Axen and Rudquist plan the nature of their intersecting elements where tension and integrity are the two components creating balance in a symbiotic relation of push and pull. The objective on this project was to communicate how the tensegrity structure tries to find the most energy-efficient solution and how external forces applied within the system are dissipated throughout so that the weak link is protected.

Axen and Rudquist plan their steady-cam shooting activity. Both artists were attached to the structure as two struts symbolising both human interference and the effects on balance. An important part was to show the shock-absorbing function of the tensegrity principle.

PRACTICE

—

Ultimately, outside the hierarchical studio project, or the established production pipeline, which have very clearly designated roles and functions, animation remains a highly specific model of expression, profoundly determined by the practice defined by the animator or artist. While traditional models of live-action production development are often predicated on the determining aspects of a conventional script – descriptive text and dialogue, influenced by narrative demands, plot, theme, genre, etc – animation is predicated on the choice of its technique, the particular material resources associated with that technique, its production process, and most importantly, its model of visualisation.

In this the animator can consider the core conditions of animation itself:

—

the use of metamorphosis;

—

the condensation of suggesting the maximum effect in the minimum of imagery;

—

the fabrication of alternative environments;

—

the use of symbol and metaphor, as well as associative idioms;

—

the penetrative illustration and interpretation of interior states, whether organic, mechanistic, or psychosomatic;

—

the anthropomorphic imposition of human traits and tropes, and

—

the resonant impact of sound.

The animator is defined by practice; practice is defined by the animator. Each practice is a re-imagining of the last, and the first of a particular level of engagement and desire.

PRAC

—
—
—
—
—

KEYWORDS IN THIS SECTION

The animated language
This discussion argues that animation is
a distinctive language, informed by the
characteristics outlined here, but also by
the qualities of re-historicisation, and the
capacity to interrogate all the assumptions
embedded in photorealistic practices. Most
importantly, animation is informed by the
stance of the creator and the way that the
practice reflects intrinsic concerns, which
could not be expressed in another form.

Creativity
Creativity is a largely taken-for-granted
aspect of the process when talking about
artistic activity. It is essentially a given
element informing any arts-based practice.
It is worth stressing that creativity in the
development of the animated form operates at
any level; it is not merely an imaginative
process, but one that involves problem-
solving, technical choices and applications,
and the ability to extrapolate concepts
into a model of visualisation, which must
necessarily move, change, and advance.
The language of animation and its cross-
disciplinary and multidisciplinary
versatility readily facilitate this.

Ultimately, outs
project, or the e
pipeline, which h
roles and functi
highly specific m
profoundly deter
defined by the a
traditional mode
development are
determining asp
script – descript
influenced by na
theme, genre, et
on the choice of
material resourc
technique, its pr
importantly, its n

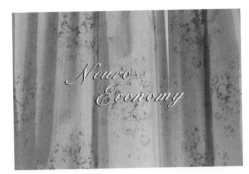

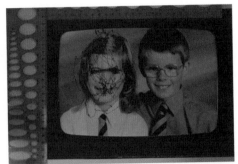

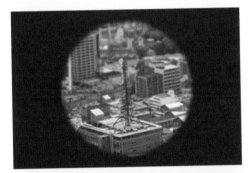

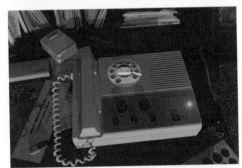

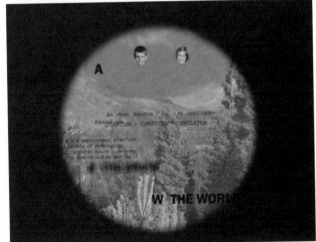

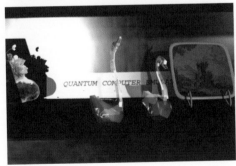

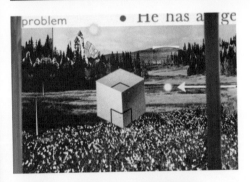

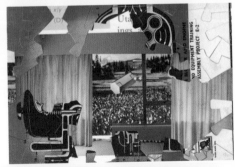

Jill Kennedy's **Neuro-Economy** is an engaging exploration of contemporary themes concerning surveillance, paranoia, the tensions between nature, suburbia, and psychological torment, and ultimately, art, culture and science.

An anonymous phone caller details his plans for a quantum computer emulator to someone he has known years previously. His message becomes the voiceover to a visual exploration of his paranoid science - the invention of the 'neuro-economy' largely expressed through 1950s and 1960s info-graphics. This is juxtaposed with images of physical and 'animal' life - underlying forces that are safely managed and sanitised by contemporary suburbia. The receiver of the call remains absent, but a connection with the caller is implied, and an uneasy correspondence informs the unfolding narrative. The images themselves become the 'neuro-economy' of the piece, illustrating animation's inherent capacity to show psychological and emotional 'interiors' and to foreground the explicit language detailed on the previous page.

01   Teaching moving image culture
02   The politics of practice
03   Animation re-imagined
04   'Object React'
05   From ideas to idioms

152/153

FROM IDEAS TO IDIOMS

05

FRO
TO

OBJECTS
OF DESIRE

In any artistic practice, the process by which an idea can be developed, enhanced and executed in a creative form is complex and demanding. The desire to express something has to be translated into a particular idiom and, as is clear from the work already presented in this discussion, this can be achieved in a variety of ways. The task of deliberating upon the best method and technique by which an idea can be expressed is at the heart of the animation process, simply because the animated form is so versatile and it can accommodate any approach that can be imagined and facilitated.

Although some critics maintain that keeping animation as a separate category from other kinds of cinema is unproductive, especially in an era in which film-makers and animators are essentially using the same digital tools and adopting many of the same processes in the creation of moving images, it is still the case that animation possesses its own distinctive vocabulary. Its applications still represent the most direct sense of the artist's intention and work as a hard copy record of psychological, emotional and somatic memory.

Animation has always been intrinsically bound up with other art forms and disciplines. Any one animated film can embrace a number of approaches: it can either reflect the expertise of the artist in a particular idiom; form a particular disciplinary background; or demonstrate how painting, sculpture, dance, drawing, making and using 3D materials, literature, etc can be used and revealed through animation. Many individual artists, in attempting to achieve the 'object of desire' – the final artefact of their practice – are constantly investigating the properties of their medium. They use animation as an interrogative tool; a tool of continuity in translating one form to another; or to adapt ideas to the visual praxis chosen as the mediator of creative expression and experience.

The above will become evident in the following examples, wherein animation is used to complement and extend works of art, such as poetry and film. Such works remain experimental and resist closure in the sense that the approach to animation in this context is one that aims to take established materials and idioms and re-engage with them aesthetically, technically, and procedurally to advance and enhance the meanings of original texts. This also foregrounds the particular interests and outlooks of the artist using the material.

Chapter 05   —
              Objects of desire
              Impossibly real
              Themes and dreams

              —
              154/155

**OBJE
OF DE**

—

—
—
—
—
—

KEYWORDS IN THIS SECTION

Memory
Animation represents a particular
opportunity to both record the act of
creative practice and to represent the
act of creative practice. The execution
of animation in any technique essentially
mediates the technical memory embedded
in the creative consciousness and the body
itself. The content of the work may also
act as a direct expression of memory, by
operating as a representation of fantasy,
feeling, recollection, preoccupation, etc.
Animation can capture inner states of
consciousness and the physical ways in
which they are expressed.

Adaptation
Animation operates as a particularly
effective tool in the translation and
adaptation of other art forms and idioms.
It extracts the essential meanings and
effects of other disciplines and advances
them through motion-driven visualisation.
Animation helps to self-consciously reveal
the movement in static forms; the purpose
and function of movement in motion forms;
and the emotive and philosophical
underpinning in text-based arts.

In any artistic p
an idea can be d
executed in a cre
demanding. The
has to be transla
and, as is clear f
presented in this
achieved in a var
of deliberating u
technique by wh
is at the heart of
simply because t
so versatile and
any approach tha
and facilitated.

maintain that kee
separate categor
cinema is unprod
era in which film
are essentially us
and adopting ma
in the creation of
the case that ani
distinctive vocabu
represent the mo
artist's intention
record of psychol
somatic memory.

05

RE-INVENTING FILM
—

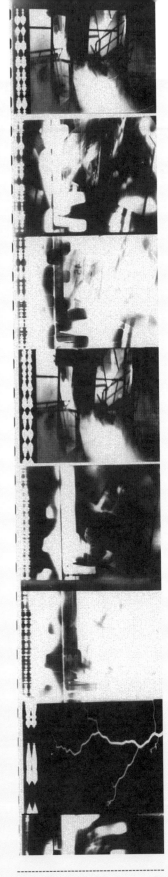

Peter Tscherkassky is an experimental film-maker who may not immediately be viewed as an animator, or indeed, working out of a fine art tradition. Much of his work is in effect a form of animation, particularly in the frame-by-frame construction of particular narratives. Most importantly, animation is also apparent in the re-invention of his films as a model by which meaning and effect is directly experienced.

RE-ANIMATION
—

He notes: 'I'm not sure I'm really interested in the question of genres and sub-genres, but I do indeed utilise a frame-by-frame technique, which could be seen in the tradition of pixellation; I use pre-existing film frames as material, which in themselves are still pictures. In this sense, you might think of my films as animated still frames and as such, as animation films'.

It is in this particular use of found footage that Tscherkassky's work as a re-animator is especially evident: 'I think the first time I used found footage as part of my own film-making process was in **Freeze Frame**. I had a cheesy little Super 8 version of an old, silent, Hollywood film called **Kreuzritter im fremden Land**, which means "crusaders in a foreign country". It depicts a crusade and "liberation" of Jerusalem. I lifted a sequence in which a young, beautiful, blonde Christian woman is being sold at a slave market. I immediately loved the idea of doing something parallel by "kidnapping" foreign pictures and using them for my own purpose, like the barbarian who kidnaps the beautiful woman, but I never intended to become a "pure" found-footage film-maker.

If I have to think of a good reason for working with found footage, I would say that I love the limitations of the given material: instead of constantly making choices of what to film, what not to film, how long to let the camera roll, etc, you have to explore a pre-existing structure, and you have to discover what is already there.'

Tscherkassky's 'kidnap' of material and his engagement with the re-imagining of the footage before him enables him to re-animate not merely the film itself, but the potential implications of its content, both formally and narratively.

In **Happy End**, he re-creates a couple's life, epitomised through their home movies. Tscherkassky relates the story of the film: 'Austrian film-maker Lisl Ponger discovered these films at a flea market and gave me the material. They were home movies in which a couple filmed themselves while celebrating events such as Christmas and birthdays. There were hours of footage with them on vacation, with friends or travelling on their own.

'My film shows a couple having big fun and enjoying life in a very particular, very Austrian kind of way. I wanted to give them a kind of resurrection. You might summarise my message to the audience as "enjoy your life in an ecstatic way, and don't forget that it will end".'

There is a great deal of pathos in the way that the couple have been given life by the omnipotence of the film-maker – he re-constructs the couple's celebrations as evidence of life-led, only for the main characters to literally fade away at the film's conclusion.

Peter Tscherkassky
re-animates found footage
in a spirit of challenging
classical Hollywood narrative
and visual composition. **Outer Space** uses film itself to
intervene with Hollywood
conventions of storytelling
and visual representation.

Chapter 05   Objects of desire   Re-inventing film   156/157
                Impossibly real
                Themes and dreams

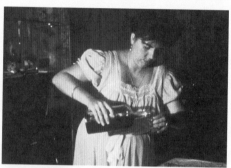

These three images were drawn
from the amateur home movies
of an unknown Austrian
couple, who record their
passing years through images
of celebration. Tscherkassky
re-animates not merely the
frames of the found footage,
but also the couple's lives
as abstract individuals
symbolising the common
experience of an existence
which relentlessly moves
through rituals such as
birthdays, weddings, public
holidays and ultimately,
death itself.

THE REPRESENTATION OF WOMEN
—

Another of Tscherkassky's found footage re-animations is **Outer Space**, a complex re-working of the B-movie horror, **The Entity**. It challenges both the generic conventions of Hollywood films, and the complacency of contemporary film in its depiction of sexual violence. Tscherkassky explains: '**Outer Space** was the third film I made in the darkroom; my second film utilising multiple layers of found source material; and the first film where I used a laser pointer to create these layerings. The leading idea was to create a film in which the filmic material itself is the main player acting in an entirely new narrative. The invisible ghost character from **The Entity** is replaced by the filmic material itself (in the form of sprocket holes, optical soundtrack, torn film strips, scratches, dirt, etc). The victim defends herself and strikes back, ultimately victorious in destroying the homogeneous, perspectively organised picture which captured her: at the very end she is the one who looks straight back into the eyes of the audience, no longer an object of the voyeuristic gaze, but a subject in her own right.'

This tour de force of re-animation effectively anthropomorphises the film material itself as the brutalising sexual and social force, which misrepresents women and female identity. The heroine's victory over the cinematic apparatus itself is also a triumph for the freedoms of animation in re-configuring conventional film form.

ANALOGUE CINEMA
—

Tscherkassky's career has embraced changes in film technology and demonstrates a profound investment in the materiality of film itself. He notes that: 'If you are interested in moving images as an art form, the materiality of the medium becomes extremely important. Modern art in general is concerned with reflections upon its materials. You can construe the birth of modern art at the end of the nineteenth century as being the result of a kind of material self-reflection, and the discovery of very specific possibilities and limitations inherent to the materials of the different art forms. In this sense, analog film and digital video have nothing to do with each other. So, basically, what I am trying to do is to create films that could only be done with film, not with the computer or a regular video camera, to show the unique possibilities of analogue cinema, which cannot be replaced by the computer. It's a swan song for classical cinema, since analogue cinema will be gone in the very near future.'

There will be film material, there will be film labs where you can print your films, but the only place where projectors will survive is the cinemathéques. These will be the last remaining places where you can show analogue films in the way they should be seen.
Peter Tscherkassky

Chapter 05   Objects of desire   Re-inventing film   158/159
                Impossibly real
                Themes and dreams

In **Outer Space**, Tscherkassky
uses the re-animation of
B-Movie Hollywood footage
to interrogate the
representation of women.
Here, he uses close-ups on
fragmentary parts of the
female body in conventional
classical cinema, with
multiple images of the
heroine (Barbara Hershey),
which suggest her
psychological state as
she seeks to defy and
resist an invisible force.

The heroine fights with
an invisible entity, but
Tscherkassky substitutes
the material of film itself
as her 'rapist', critiquing
mainstream cinema's use of
women as sexual objects.

The material of film stock
is animated as the subject
of the piece, violently
ripping and tearing its
way through notions of
narrative; it becomes an
all-encompassing abstract
force of representation
and intervention.

RE-IMAGINING POETRY

—

A number of animators have identified a link between the poem and the animated form. In general, animation and poetry can share some similar and pertinent characteristics. Often, both occur in short form and use language to either condense or suggest meaning. Both forms are also informed by the self-reflexive presence of the author. Animation and poetry also deliberately play with established codes and conventions of expression and visualisation. Both maintain an openness to interpretation through the various layers of meaning embedded in the literal execution of the message and material expressed. The following is an example of a poem expressed and re-invented using the animation medium.

```
Forgetfulness
By Billy Collins

The name of the author is the first to go
followed obediently by the title, the plot,
the heartbreaking conclusion, the entire novel
which suddenly becomes one you have never read, never even heard of,

as if, one by one, the memories you used to harbor
decided to retire to the southern hemisphere of the brain,
to a little fishing village where there are no phones.

Long ago you kissed the names of the nine muses goodbye
and watched the quadratic equation pack its bag,
and even now as you memorize the order of the planets,

something else is slipping away, a state flower perhaps,
the address of an uncle, the capital of Paraguay.

Whatever it is you are struggling to remember,
it is not poised on the tip of your tongue
or even lurking in some obscure corner of your spleen.

It has floated away down a dark mythological river
whose name begins with an L as far as you can recall

on your own way to oblivion where you will join those
who have even forgotten how to swim and how to ride a bicycle.

No wonder you rise in the middle of the night
to look up the date of a famous battle in a book on war.
No wonder the moon in the window seems to have drifted
out of a love poem that you used to know by heart.
```

Billy Collins, 'Forgetfulness' from **Questions About Angels**. Copyright 1999 by Billy Collins. Reprinted with the permission of University of Pittsburgh Press.

Chapter 05   Objects of desire   Re-imagining poetry   160/161
                     Impossibly real
                     Themes and dreams

Julian Grey of Head Gear Animation has embraced the special relationship between poetry and animation in his interpretation of ex-USA Poet Laureate, Billy Collins's work 'Forgetfulness'.

It is a wistful look at the seemingly ever-reducing capacity for particular kinds of factual, and ultimately emotional, memory to fade with the aging process. Grey cleverly uses animation's capacity for erasure to interpret Collins's work, stripping novels of their spines and inner pages therefore rendering them as both white spaces and evidence of absence – modernist idioms of unrecognised or ignored latent potential. As the implied figure in the poem moves away from the bookshop, lost memories are depicted as fading and migrating birds, while the more literally visualised aspects of our recollection and experience are deconstructed and disappear. The pictorial and the graphic – photographs, maps, handmade objects – flicker intermittently as signifiers of recall, but they also fade or float away. The audience is faced with the inevitability of acknowledging lost motor skills and intuitive practices; the desperate attempt at verification of experience; and the ultimate acceptance of lost love and possibility.

The animated film **Forgetfulness** was commissioned by the advertising agency J Walter Thompson in New York on behalf of the Sundance Channel for its Action Poetry Series. Grey decided to make three titles for the series, with each chosen poem suggesting different animation styles and approaches. The aesthetic look of Super 8 scratchy film was crucial to the project. It was a key metaphor for memory in **Forgetfulness** and in Grey's view a huge reservoir of personal memory as home movies from the 1960s and 1970s.

In approaching the subject matter of the poem, Grey was particularly responsive to Collins's delivery of his own work: 'Collins's wry wit and dry delivery are qualities I readily respond to. His approach, though contemplative, is matter-of-fact and unadorned. I attempted to represent his words visually in the same manner, with imagery that was at once mundane, beautiful and whimsical'.

Grey wanted to let the poem speak for itself, but sought to visually represent what he imagined as he heard Collins read the poem and hoped that this resonated with others who knew it or are hearing it for the first time. Crucially, he wanted to pique the interest of otherwise disinterested viewers and listeners by using a visual medium to engage them with the art.

Grey is encouraged by the ways in which animation can now reach a variety of audiences, but also by the fact that almost anyone can create moving-image work: 'Today animation crosses boundaries of art and commerce, analogue and digital, slickness and roughness. As well, more and more people are incorporating animated elements within otherwise non-animated pieces. I am very much informed by the work of my industry peers. With the advent of YouTube and websites delivering hi-res quicktimes of the latest spots and videos, it is easy to be exposed to the best and boldest, commercial and not, which can only have the effect of advancing the medium into new territory.'

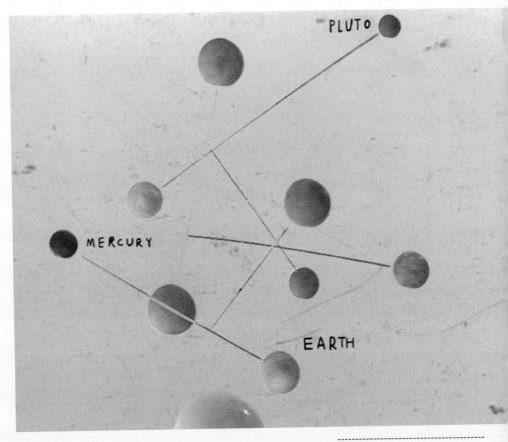

At school, we are often taught core concepts and ideas through graphic idioms such as charts and maps, and our memory of the ideas and concepts is often prompted by the ways that they have been visualised. Grey depicts Collins's attempt to memorise the order of the planets in the solar system in this way.

Chapter 05   — Objects of desire   — Re-imagining poetry   — 162/163
                    Impossibly real
                    Themes and dreams

With the advent of websites delivering hi-res quicktimes, it is easy to be exposed to the best and boldest, which can only have the effect of advancing the medium into new territory.
Julian Grey

Grey uses an erasure technique to show our fading memories of childhood and our loss of motor skills. These are evident in his depictions of the act of swimming and the slow alienation from our bodies and emotions. Collins's lyricism and Grey's clever sensitivity to the wistful acceptance of these realities both offer up a pertinent insight into the power and effect of memories, and animation acts as an adaptable and adaptive tool of expression.

Grey depicts our memories as imaginary sailing ships in a way in which we might actually make and conceive of them as paper boats.

IMPOSSIBLY REAL

—

Contemporary animation in all its guises ironically follows the same trajectory of many former developments in the form by aping photorealism and the relentless drive to reproduce reality, and facilitating fantastical figures, landscapes and forms – the art of the impossible. What seems clear, though, is that the pictorial realms of the imagination, the parameters of surreal fantasy, and the visual signifiers of spontaneity, are increasingly controlled, measured and authenticated as if they were real. Essentially, all accepted knowledge about something is challenged by using animation. All supposed objective knowledge is made subjective and shown in a different light. However something may have been perceived or received can be subject to change.

Ironically, Gollum, WETA Digital's highly persuasive computer-generated character, is as real as their equally fabricated, but partially referential, King Kong. Both characters in turn function on the same plane as Robert de Niro or Meryl Streep, the last great purveyors of method acting, wherein the model of performance is based on the greatest degree of physical and psychological empathy and immersion. For every assumption of cinematic truth, there is the acknowledgement of animated artifice; for the apparently real, there is little reality apparent. The extended degree of constructedness in the real, and the ways that this has been used to authenticate even the most extreme of fantasy narratives, has left a challenge for animators to reinvent and re-imagine spectacle.

Chapter 05   Objects of desire
                Impossibly real
                Themes and dreams

164/165

IMPO
REAL

—

KEYWORDS IN THIS SECTION

Realism

There remains great irony in the fact that
animation, surely the natural language of
imaginative and fantastical expression, is
often seen at its most persuasive and
effective when aspiring to imitate the
photorealistic. Creating a fully plausible,
realistically rendered human being remains
a holy grail for animators and visual effects
artists, while dinosaurs, mythical creatures
and ogres - the very stuff of fantasy - are
seen to be animated in as realistic a way as
can be achieved. Such is the sophistication
of the contemporary viewer; the real
challenge for many artists is to achieve
the 'impossibly real' to ensure the
suspension of disbelief.

Spectacle

There is further irony that special effects
are really no longer special. As there are
so many animated effects in Hollywood cinema,
there is a strong argument that traditional
live action may be understood as a model of
animation. Spectacle is a taken-for-granted
aspect of many narratives, but its meaning
and effect are at best visceral, at worst,
numbing and without impact. While animation
may be an effective tool in its achievement,
many questions might be asked of its purpose
and the politics it supports or obscures.

Contemporary a
ironically follow
many former de
by aping photore
drive to reprodu
fantastical figur
the art of the im
though, is that th
imagination, the
fantasy, and the
spontaneity, are
measured and au
real. Essentially,
about something
animation. All su
is made subjectiv
light. However sc
perceived or rece
to change.

05

Andy Huang's extraordinary short, **Doll Face**, explores the fate of a machine as it seeks to create its own identity. With nods to **Metropolis** and **Ghost in the Shell**, Huang creates a part-human, part-machine figure, which emerges out of a metal box seeking to copy TV images of a beautiful woman with a made-up face. The machine assumes that the image on the television is both real and the ideal - an inspiring icon it should ape and aspire to.

The machine operates as a parody of the constructed nature of physical, material and psychological identity in the contemporary era, as it seeks to create an illusional and delusional beauty through make-up.

The machine figure precariously reaches out of its box to reach an even greater closeness and empathy with the TV set; it is desperate to understand and embrace its sense of the 'impossibly real'.

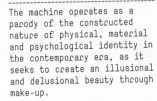

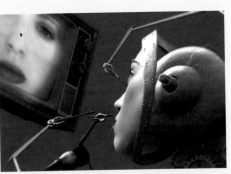

The idyllic qualities captured in the imagery of advertising create a false consciousness in those who aspire to copy it. In essence, commercial culture ultimately creates unattainable fantasy worlds.

The machine over-reaches in its desire to touch the TV image and is ultimately destroyed. The face falls and breaks apart, revealing the hollowness of the image. This symbolises the meaningless aspiration in securing contemporary notions of identity.

Chapter 05   Objects of desire   Re-imagining spectacle I   166/167
                Impossibly real
                Themes and dreams

RE-IMAGINING SPECTACLE I

The Fallon Agency's colourful Play-Doh advertisement for Sony Bravia television, returns to the traditional form of 3D stop-motion animation using clay-animated sculptures of rabbits, whales and cubic forms to re-invent a city landscape, which draws attention to the scale of the animation. The promotion of the ad sought to stress its craft elements and the distinctly hands-on approach of its 40 animators working with 40 tonnes of clay in a sweltering environment to create 100,000 single images, which were later animated in a traditional frame-by-frame method. Here, a small-scale technique is being played out on a literally unimaginable scale even to those consistently working in the 3D stop-motion form.

Sony's previous TV ads feature millions of coloured balls bouncing down the road, and a paint explosion throughout an abandoned block of flats. Animation director, Darren Walsh, stresses the material and the tactile, and ironically, implies a mistrust of the plastic illusionism of the dominant aesthetics of the computer-generated image. The return to a physical material is seemingly a return to the real, even if it is subject to the same manipulation.

Numerous 3D stop-motion animated rabbits populate a city environment, all invoking nature, suggesting the child's playroom and engaging with the kitsch juxtapositions of late pop art.

The leaping animated rabbits at once signify their artifice as stop-motion figures, while suggesting a real, tangible presence as an object.

The juxtaposition between humankind and the artificial rabbits suggests estrangement between humankind and animals; it is in some ways re-invoked through the symbolic nature of the imagery.

The Play-Doh ad seeks to imply the investment in the craft element of the preparation of the material, and the sense of tactility and presence of the objects, particularly through their unusual scale.

The Play-Doh cubes make reference to abstract conceptions of animated choreography and show the building-block aspect of the city by alluding to the frame-by-frame building block construction of the piece.

The sense of scale is also conveyed through the iconic use of billboards and the city skyline. Big, in this sense, is inevitably more beautiful, because ironically it relates to the notion of small.

RE-IMAGINING SPECTACLE II

—

Emerging as a major talent in animation through the popularity of his films online, PES has already received major recognition for his re-imagining of everyday objects. His films are mini-masterpieces of condensation and symbolic association. PES's extraordinary eye for seeing a resonant resemblance or action in an object enables him to successfully re-invent genre, and most importantly, re-imagine the material space of his narratives in an entirely original way. His two most notable films, **Roof Sex** and **KaBoom!**, demonstrate the very opposite of the Play-Doh ads by making the viewer consider the minutiae of objects as they resonate with narrative, contextual and conceptual associations.

Roof Sex features two chairs having sex on a New York roof. It plays with the surreal and amusing parameters of 'furniture porn', linking the often gendered nature of furniture, with its anthropomorphised legs, arms and backs, to the assumption that such furniture might have sex. PES researched material using furniture porn sites, featuring a variety of chairs in provocative positions. He taught himself to animate chairs by practising with doll-house furniture.

Having fully storyboarded the sequence, he animated **Roof Sex** by featuring a gold and a red chair. Both chairs adopt a variety of sexual positions and vigorously squeal and shout until orgasm. Later in the film, an old granny discovers the inevitably damaged chairs in her living room and hits the cat with a broom, believing it had caused the rips and tears on the chairs.

PES's skills in seeing the associations between objects is at its keenest in his film **KaBoom!** – an implicitly anti-war tract that makes comment upon the perversity of America's war in Iraq. The film features the bombing of a quasi-Iraqi, retro-futuristic city, but the appeal is in the detail and the symbolic resonance of the associative images.

The film began as a consequence of an electrical fire in PES's apartment, which caused a power surge that destroyed many of his household appliances. Removing the circuit boards from his computers, he noticed that they resembled cities when viewed from above. He then proceeded to create the city with old objects such as razors and drill bits. Glass, plastic and metal all ape modernist conceptions of past architectures. The guns that defend the city are old skeleton keys with wide barrels. Popcorn plays the part of anti-aircraft fire; a vintage-blue toy bomber, augmented with matchstick missiles with cotton wool, smoke-stream bombs the city; while the bomb is played by a peanut.

PES notes: 'Apparently the atomic bomb has a peanut structure with two compartments. I always found it ironic that while bombing was occurring, a few hundred miles away would be the dropping of care packages to those that had just been bombed, and it would always include peanut butter because it was so rich in protein. The peanut seems like the closest thing to a Christmas gift, too. It has outside packaging, and a tissue-like inner layer; it's a pretty ironic gift in the film though'. Yellow gift bows double as explosions ballooning out upon impact, while 1950s Christmas baubles

PES shoots some of his first stop-motion sequences of 'chair-on-chair' sexual activity, relying on days with clear blue skies in order to evoke the brightly lit, cubist clarities of traditional American comic books.

PES choreographs two chairs having sex on a roof. In spite of the obvious comic artifice involved, and the surreal parody of performance in pornographic material, viewers have still reported arousal and guilt as they watched the film on their office computers!

Chapter 05   Objects of desire   Re-imagining spectacle II   168/169
             Impossibly real
             Themes and dreams

feature in the final destruction of the city suggesting not only an atomic blast, but also the effects of chemical and germ warfare. These objects, while having a literal association, are also inevitably ironic – their very commonness subverts the scale of the subject matter being dealt with. The act of war is made ridiculous by the trivial and celebratory artefacts that represent it.

The final associations emerge from the film's title. **KaBoom!** is named after a 1970s breakfast cereal featuring sugar clown-heads, and an Atari video game with a character called 'the mad bomber', whose only function was to drop bombs. The George Bush analogy need not be overstated.

PES's vintage-blue toy bomber, with its matchstick missiles, bombs a city-like circuit board torn from a computer. In such images, the politics of war are readily evoked. War is paralleled to a child's game; the childishness is implied in the ease with which conflict is engaged and the distance politicians have from the consequences of their decisions.

PES's retro-futuristic city made of household items, is an invocation of modernist architecture and a reference to the cliché of the minaretted skylines that allude to the Middle East.

PES uses household objects and familiar materials to create his own version of the PacMan and Space Invaders games. This playfulness with objects draws attention to their taken-for-granted functions and meanings and challenges them.

THEMES AND DREAMS

A true revolution within animation is impending, and like all revolutions in animation, it will be technological. Even the briefest survey of motion technologies suggests that animation will be reconfigured in all manner of new contexts and environments. For example, a software application called Seadragon enables users to seamlessly and instantly view and access high resolution data as effortlessly as one might view thumbnails on the Internet. The intention is to enable the user to browse vast amounts of data smoothly. This software will revolutionise the way we use screens, and therefore, the way content is developed and delivered for screen use.

Seadragon and other similar developments look set to reinvent screen-based media, facilitating a further dimension of depth to animation, and a resultant level of interactivity. Users will be able to scour and inspect animated media, much as one might marvel at a mediaeval miniature.

The screen, of course, is already being reinvented. Jeff Han's touch-based, pressure-sensitive multi-user scaleable touch interface is a prime example of the desire to move away from preset directorial narrative in preference of an immersive and interactive animated experience. This can be seen in a simpler form within Apple's iPhone or Microsoft's Surface. Han's animated 'swimming portal' enables the user to figuratively swim within any scene and explore it. However, it is clear that the re-imagining of animation will get particularly interesting when software such as Seadragon is used in conjunction with multi-user touch-screen technology, and the newly developed Photosynth (Microsoft Live Labs) program.

Photosynth builds visual environments from materials posted online and maps social data three-dimensionally via meta tags. This then creates a full 3D social experience – Metaverse – a global cross-modal/cross-user social experience built on hyperlinks. The implications for animation are potentially vast. Photography is used to construct malleable global models of virtually everything photographed and posted online, and via Seadragon, there is the possibility to explore to a seamlessly indefinite depth.

Chapter 05   Objects of desire
             Impossibly real
             Themes and dreams

170/171

THEM
DREA

Interactivity

For a long time, the 'convergence' of
disciplines and technologies has promised
various kinds of interactive, immersive
experience, in which the act of animation
becomes one and the same as the consequence
of the action executed. Interactivity enables
the user to animate, as much as the animator
has enabled the tools to be animated. The
user becomes the author.

Human performance

At the centre of the re-animation of the
form, will be the ways in which technology
empowers humankind not merely to use the
tools in playing out the functions of
expression, but in the ways that the
body itself will play a singular part
in performing the act of animation within
an immersive space. This in itself will
re-invoke 'nature', and potentially change
its conditions.

A true revolution
impending, and l
animation, it wil
the briefest surv
suggests that ar
in all manner of
environments. Fo
application calle
to seamlessly ar
high resolution d
might view thum
intention is to en
amounts of data
revolutionise the
therefore, the wa
delivered for scr

developments lo
based media, fac
of depth to anima
interactivity. Use
inspect animated
marvel at a medi

already being rei
based, pressure-s
scaleable touch i

05

Essentially, it is a global social diorama, a semantic network, that as an experience will render the one-way traffic of animated cinematic narrative an archaic, impotent and, ultimately, joyless experience.

REVOLUTIONISING ANIMATION
—

Research started within the Massachusetts Institute of Technology, and is now progressing rapidly and widely. It looks set to dramatically reinvent and revolutionise animation, through the removal of the screen and the director's emphatic voice in the delivery of real time physical interaction. The death of the screen would inevitably re-imagine animation. The use of Wii technology in the generation of social animation experiences is already occurring.

This potential shift away from not only the screen, but also the browser, creates a space between the real and the virtual that animation looks set to fill, delivering shared, communal, animated experiences. Already the individual, or more often the consumer, is becoming accustomed to directing and controlling animation that is aimed at them. Adobe has already been using interactive advertising hoarding technology to promote its software packages in New York; the target audiences use their own body movements to dictate the pace of the ad, the direction that the animation runs in, and ultimately, to engage with its message. Photography is no longer the index of the real – our gestures and performances, as in the Wii, are much more an index of the real. Humankind learns gestural icons through the performance of the real. Whilst it is a simulatory culture, we are in it, and we are performing within it. Look at how children interact with the Wii. They don't need the reality that adults seek.

As photography cannot render a malleable three-dimensionality, the visual language of moving image communication will be 3D CGI animation and the physical and material technologies, which become the signifiers of the personalised animation of change. The 2D screen, the frame, the one-way communication, the depth (interestingly, resolution will no longer be fixed but rather explorable deep space) the emphatic narrative – all will be rendered archaic. Doubtless, this too, will be re-imagined in response. Animation simply begets animation.

Chapter 05   Objects of desire
             Impossibly real
             Themes and dreams

                                                    172/173

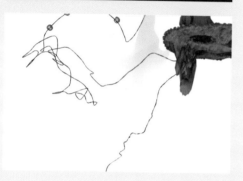

In his films, Robert Seidel is interested in pushing the boundaries of organic beauty and emotions with technology. He is inspired by the complexity of nature, a childhood fascination for Eastern European animation, the endless digital possibilities and the subtlety of fine art. His movies grow out of initial paintings and sketches. These get animated with visual and scientific software to create 'living paintings', which connect with the viewer on an unconscious level.

His movie, **Grau**, is a personal reflection on the memories that come up during a car accident. Real events from the past are visualised by merging, fusing and eroding 'biographical sculptures'- partly based on three-dimensional scans, motion capture data and x-rays. These artefacts create a very intimate snapshot of a whole life within its last split seconds.

In Seidel's installation-based works, here represented by **Dive Painting**, he extends his canvas to large screens and architectural projections. By putting the façade of a natural history museum in motion, he frees animation to explore a new relationship of size, scale and texture - layering them to a unique expressive experience.

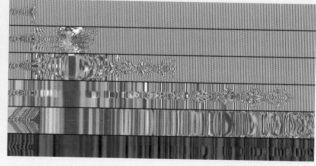

RE-IMAGINING NATURE

—

Karolina Sobecka's **Wildlife** project is a challenging engagement with the overlooked aspects of urban orthodoxy and the increasing absence of the animal from human cultures. She explains: 'I want to wake people's sense of wonder, make them look at the world anew, become children again and see a world in which anything can still happen. This work is a constructed (both literally and metaphorically) environment, which results in a distorted and confused concept of our relationship with nature. I was developing the idea of movement through space, which becomes a movement through a film, and through a narrative and cinematic space.

'My first approach was to position actual frames (physical signs) along the road. This, of course, was not very feasible, both for practical reasons and because of the fact that this method wouldn't really create continuous cinematic space. While doing my research, I discovered Bill Brand's **Masstransiscope** – a mural in a New York subway system that works like a zoetrope, and is animated by the movement of passing trains. Brand actually installed a series of vertical slits in an abandoned subway station through which people would glimpse the paintings on the wall of the station. This work provided an inspiration for creating a mechanism that would provide a similar effect, but would be self-contained –

images would be projected from the moving object itself. I decided to link the movement of the car through space to the movement through time in a film. I considered using a GPS module, but eventually settled on monitoring the car's speed, which allowed for greater responsiveness. At the same time, I was also thinking about the content for this interface, one that would both resonate with the urban environment and with the delivery method.'

Sobecka chose to situate the work in this way, in order to redefine urban elements as proto-animation, and demonstrate everyday kinesis captured in more formal animated forms: 'The idea of the movement of the car animating through sequences of images seemed particularly fitting since the car is already almost a cinematic device by itself. It is like an internal capsule separated from reality. When we're sitting in the car looking out the window, what we experience is very much like what we experience in a movie theatre. The window forms a screen, physically limited on all sides. We're seated and not part of the space we're looking out on. We are also in a kind of transitory space, literally in-between two places, and also half in our internal world, usually lost in our thoughts, while still in physical reality. This corresponds to my interest in "augmented reality" – blends of the virtual and physical.

We're seated, not part of the space we're looking out on. We are also in a kind of transitory space, literally in-between two places, and also half in our internal world, usually lost in our thoughts, while still in physical reality.
Karolina Sobecka

Chapter 05   Objects of desire   Re-imagining nature   174/175
             Impossibly real
             Themes and dreams

The fact that **Wildlife** existed out in the city, in people's everyday reality, is also very important to me. I wanted it to exist as a layer interjected into reality and experienced by anybody going about their regular day. It only gains its meaning outside of the context of a gallery space or a movie theatre. The urban context is an active element in the work and in a large part forms the meaning of the piece. It contributes to the metaphor as a "constructed" environment that forms the support for our conceptual projections.'
           Interestingly, though Sobecka sought to animate and augment, she found that the urban space had already been colonised by animated augmentations.

In Karolina Sobecka's
Wildlife installation,
a moving image of a tiger
in the urban landscape is
prompted by a car sensor.
It seeks to re-awaken what
she views as 'the ability to
see things' in the overloaded
sensory and social spaces
of contemporary city life.

AUGMENTED REALITY
—

'I didn't anticipate how much people have already adapted to a certain kind of augmented reality – to images and light movement on the streets, due to the spread of advertising. Some people would simply not notice the tiger. The most magical spaces were created in areas with the absence of advertising, such as the mostly abandoned, industrial downtown Los Angeles. Dark and nostalgic buildings were perfect support for the projection; the disillusioned and the homeless the ideal audience. Groups of youths on cruiser bikes also welcomed the fantastic creature. I'm interested in the relationship between humankind, technology and nature. It is very difficult to understand our place in it.

'Cities still shelter us from nature, although it is perhaps nature that now needs to be protected from the encroachment of culture. Most creatures that once threatened our survival are endangered now, victims of the spell they still hold over us. It is estimated that there are now more privately owned tigers than in the wild. The owners often see themselves as the 'saviours' of the animals; some are just giving in to the age-old fascination with them. One of the responses I got from someone who saw **Wildlife** is an example of a start of a dialogue that I would like to catalyse: "How fitting that an illusion from a car is all we will probably ever know about the wildlife we are killing with our fossil fuels, oil wars, and rampant overuse of the earth's resources."

'It is sad that the grandeur of large dangerous animals is lost and compromised when we see them caged and on the verge of extinction due to our conquest of nature. The issue of our relationship with nature deserves a lot of attention and perhaps **Wildlife** can serve as another voice pointing to it.'

Chapter 05   Objects of desire   Re-imagining nature   176/177
               Impossibly real
               Themes and dreams

The epic scale of the tiger
becomes an ironic artificial
imposition of lost nature in
an urban landscape; it points
out humankind's loss of its
primal bonds with animals.

The tiger sometimes shocked
and surprised passers-by.
On other occasions, it was
merely understood as part
of a possible advertising
system, evoking no reaction
or appreciation for the art
of animation.

RE-IMAGINING NURTURE

—

In 2006, HypoSurface Corp was approached by Margaret Core, Director of Sales and Marketing, Conventions and Conferences for the Biotechnology Industry Organization (BIO). Her desire was to find a way to animate the front foyer space of the BIO conference at the Boston Convention Centre – to engage the erudite audience of scientists who gather for this quiet and academic event. Professor Mark Goulthorpe showed her a small prototype of HypoSurface 2.0 at MIT's Media Lab, which gave a small hint of the capability of the new medium to provide an immersive, fully interactive event space. The first commercial prototype (HypoSurface 1.0) was installed as frontispiece of the IMTS (International Manufacturers Technology Show) in the foyer of McCormick Place, as a highly innovative and emotive display technology to stimulate discussion amongst the 100,000 engineers who visited IMTS. It became the talking point of the show – a 'live' MIT development project for the exhibitors to witness, as it evolved daily.

Professor Goulthorpe explains: 'At IMTS, HypoSurface was effectively a demonstration piece that evidenced the potency of information-bus technologies at what is the foremost showcase of digital manufacturing globally. 560 actuators were deployed at high speed in response to direct user input – the sound and movement of the visiting public. The sheer speed of digital signalling allowed highly articulate movement of the actuators, which in turn deformed a rubber/metal display surface some 2ft, deploying waves at up to 60mph! What was already apparent at IMTS, albeit in prototypical form, was the birth of a new medium – the display surface itself subject to high-speed physical movement, like waves on a lake. Only this lake, this prototypical HypoSurface, was a vertical metallic sheet that was being controlled powerfully and precisely to display text, logos, patterns, and waves, via a digital interface. Information-become-form!

This animated surface revolutionises models of signage, foregrounding its materiality and tactility as an appealing aesthetic as well as communications form. Goulthorpe notes, though: 'What was crucial was the group recognition that the potential lay in HypoSurface's broad interactive range, where multimedia channels link into its dramatic movement capacity: not as a simple visual display, but as a fully social "theatre". What emerged was a sense that a more effective strategy would be one of intrigue, where HypoSurface would be used to engage and stimulate, but not "inform" its audience – to leave them puzzled, but thrilled – left with a motivated question mark! Implicitly, this announced a perceived shift in desire and expectation of the audience itself – that a digitally connected, scientifically savvy audience required new forms of engagement that might tease at its collective erudition.

'We therefore set about devising a thematically targeted sound/movement matrix that would offer an endlessly diverse event that continually invited input from the BIO audience, constantly demanding interpretation. The HypoSurface was installed as a free-standing 33ft x 12ft metallic voxel surface.

Chapter 05   Objects of desire   —
               Impossibly real   Re-imagining nurture
               Themes and dreams   178/179

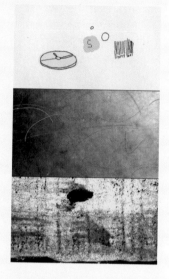

Max Hattler is interested in the space between abstraction and figuration, where storytelling is freed from the constraints of traditional narrative. His work contemplates microcosms, moments and atmospheres. While his films tend to be without dialogue, they explore the relationship between sound, music and the moving image. **Drift** sees the body as a metaphorical landscape. Eerie and sometimes too close for comfort, the film aims to transform the familiar and mundane into something poetic and mysterious in order to create distance from closeness, and reflection from immersion.

The music for **Drift** was composed by Mark Bowden. **Drift** considers the body as landscape through close-up images of skin. The music, likewise, takes a close-up view of a series of harp chords and viola harmonics. By using real photography in extreme close-up, a foreign yet familiar world is created. This tension is mirrored in the music.

Original samples are exploded into a multitude of tiny elements before being reconstructed into a tight arrangement based on the Fibonacci series. Visually, the hair floats through the landscape and creates an oblique narrative, while three layers of sound unfold concurrently, creating an evolving wave of harp and viola sounds interspersed with granulated electronic frequencies. In a different way, Hattler's outlook reflects Goulthorpe's work with HypoSurface in seeking to recall biological life to animation enterprise.

A member of the public tests the living technology, HypoSurface, both activating and responding to its 'vertical liquid' animated properties.

Adjacent to HypoSurface was a giant BIO globe offering information to the attendees as projections. LED screens, mice and scrolling menus were also available. The difference in communication logics (not just technologies) could not have been more striking. The brilliant success of HypoSurface relative to these more normative communications techniques was expressed strikingly by the globe's emptiness, it being used as seating to watch the evolving drama of the HypoSurface and its public! Information and understanding were realigned, quite literally, to the participatory multimedia theatre of HypoSurface.'

RE-INVENTING METAMORPHOSIS
—

Goulthorpe devised HypoSpace using the core principles of the emergence and reproduction of biological life; an echo of the essential animus in animation, and a prompt for metamorphosis as the condition of the surface evolution.

A crucial aspect in implying narrative and context in relation to the surface shifts was the use of sound. Goulthorpe notes: 'Our digital composer, Paul Steenhuisen, created 700 sound clips that were drawn from nature: raindrops, wood growth and destruction, breathing, frogs, roosters, dogs, cows, horses, gutteral words, etc. These sound clips were arranged as

sound sets (such as 'horse'), digitally processed from 'dry' sounds to highly processed 'wet' sounds (from 'normal' horse to 'crazy' horse). Crucial was their basic sonic coherence – that they could all be combined non-discordantly in endless combinations – as sounds in nature. We provided three microphones in front of the HypoSurface, input coming from the passing audience. Any input voice or whisper would be digitally processed and played back.

From the same input, but at a louder level, individual sounds from another of the sound sets were triggered. The more insistent the input, the more processed the output, such that a simple whisper became a crazy shout (with increased volume and feeling). Input from the three microphones continually created a densely layered, but bewitching digital/natural soundscape, sometimes with 30 or 40 layered sound files, all utterly beguiling but simultaneously hilarious. The sound system at the event grabbed people immediately and held their attention – they often participated for quite long periods of time.'

The varied dynamics of the sound inputs animated the HypoSurface in a genuine form of interactivity: 'As input comes in (from a microphone or camera), so it is analysed for content (such as volume, tone, speed), and a sound triggered from the sound sets that suits the input. The choreographic interface takes any selected movement type

Multiple-input continually created a densely layered but bewitching 'digital/natural' soundscape – utterly beguiling but simultaneously hilarious – a highly sophisticated digital 'sea' of sound.
Mark Goulthorpe

Chapter 05   Objects of desire   —
               Impossibly real   Re-imagining nurture   180/181
               Themes and dreams

and picks a correspondingly distorted math file. Quite quickly, people realised that sound input affects movement output, not just quantitatively, but qualitatively.'

The audience quickly learned to exercise the range of vocal input to test the range of the movement output, thrilled by the power of their vocality. In so doing, the system began to get more active. Further, the surface accommodated complex engagements with creating text, almost suggesting a sense of moving concrete poetry and experimental motion graphics. The HypoSurface, a shimmering and iridescent flowing form, becomes the embodiment of animated 'vertical liquid' performance, provoking a visceral experience.

Goulthorpe speculates: 'The sustained barrage of stimulation prompted intrigue: What is the sound and what is the movement? And why this text? At that point of total engagement there was extraordinary focus, attained through a quite sophisticated deployment of interactive media, but most certainly brought to a head by the simple fact of movement that seems to hypnotise even erudite audiences.'

INFORMATION WATERFALL
—

'What seemed the most intangible yet most powerful aspect of HypoSurface's success was that technology and public fused. Indeed, it was only through the engagement of the audience in its interactive systems that HypoSurface became expressive. The soundscapes and the various textual and mathematic movement sequences were released only through the audience and their communal engagement with HypoSurface. The more engaged the audience became with the HypoSurface systems, the more sophisticated the response; and the greater the degree of teamwork between the players, the greater the range of sounds effects deployed.

'The very act of participation, the "joy" of the HypoSurface's powerful responsiveness to a whisper, worked to bind a community. Such participatory theatre, enticing erudite interaction with a thrilling digital potency (an information "waterfall"), and teasing at the interpretive intellect of a now-digital audience, engendered identification of the audience with themselves; it worked by structuring identity through participation. HypoSurface seemed, in its powerfully physical presence, to condense the two great forces of our time – innovation and communication – into identity. Further, humanity itself is re-imagined as animation.'

—
Appendix

—
Conclusion
Bibliography
Further resources and webography
Index
Acknowledgements and picture credits

—
182/183

APPENDIX

—

—
Appendix

Conclusion
Bibliography
Further resources and webography
Index
Acknowledgements and picture credits

CONCLUSION

According to composer Barry Evans: 'From the layered images of Reynaud's Praxinoscope Theatre in the nineteenth century to today's digital compositing, the circle is complete. The integration of live action and "drawn" images has become commonplace. It has always been possible through optical printing, but now it is as simple as a mouse click. It has been much quoted by many that all cinema is animation. Each individual frame is editable (and usually edited), whether it is simple levels and colour correction (keyframed and then rendered frame-by-frame), composited 3D computer graphics with motion and camera tracking, or a complete virtual world running in real time on your computer or rendered frame-by-frame in high resolution for eventual digital video projection.'

However, this sense of 'full circle' in cinematic terms has only necessitated a bigger breach in the ways animation can configure itself. As Karolina Sobecka notes: 'Digital technologies are dissolving the borders between disciplinary forms. Animation techniques have been widely adopted by other cultural production areas from art to science. Even though these works are not called animations, because this term, sadly, still connotes a very narrowly understood format, this fact proves how much potential animation has as a means of expression. I think the term "animation" is still understood as relating to the craft rather than to the form of art. I also think concept is seen as a secondary concern in a work that calls itself animation.'

This discussion has sought to remedy this outlook – suggesting that animation should be seen as an art and a craft across multiple platforms and disciplines, and the tool by which art, science, culture and the human condition has been imagined and re-imagined. As animation bleeds into other areas such as machinema, games technology, interactive holograms in real time and Digital Light Processing (DLP), it is clear that the term, the process, the achievement and the outlook defining animation has been re-thought, revised and re-invented. It is likely to merely be the beginning, for in re-imagining themselves, artists, animators, practitioners, creators and moving-image manipulators, will inevitably re-imagine their tools of expression and re-engage, refresh and renew the world once more.

Appendix

Conclusion
Bibliography
Further resources and webography
Index
Acknowledgements and picture credits

184/185

BIBLIOGRAPHY

ANIMATION HISTORY

Adams, TR (1991)
Tom and Jerry: Fifty Years of Cat and Mouse
(New York: Crescent Books)

Adamson, J (1975)
Tex Avery: King of Cartoons
(New York: Da Capo)

Barrier, M (1999)
Hollywood Cartoons: American Animation in its Golden Age
(New York & Oxford: OUP)

Beck, J (1994)
The 50 Greatest Cartoons
(Atlanta: Turner Publishing Co)

Beck, J (2004)
Animation Art
(London: Harper Collins Design)

Bendazzi, G (1994)
Cartoons: One Hundred Years of Cartoon Animation
(London: John Libbey)

Brion, P (1990)
Tom and Jerry: The Definitive Guide to their Animated Adventures
(New York: Harmony)

Bruce Holman, L (1975)
Puppet Animation in the Cinema: History and Technique
(New York: AS Barnes)

Cabarga, L (1988)
The Fleischer Story
(New York: Da Capo)

Crafton, D (1993)
Before Mickey: The Animated Film, 1898-1928
(Chicago: University of Chicago Press)

Eliot, M (1994)
Walt Disney: Hollywood's Dark Prince
(London: Harper Collins Design)

Frierson, M (1994)
Clay Animation: American Highlights 1908-Present
(New York: Twayne)

Holliss, R & Sibley, B (1988)
The Disney Studio Story
(New York: Crown)

Kenner, H (1994)
Chuck Jones: A Flurry of Drawings, Portraits of American Genius
(Berkeley: University of California Press)

Lawson, T & Persons, A (2004)
The Magic Behind the Voices
(Jackson: University of Mississippi)

Maltin, L (1987)
Of Mice and Magic: A History of American Animated Cartoons
(New York: Plume)

Manvell, R (1980)
Art and Animation: The Story of Halas and Batchelor Animation Studio 1940-1980
(Keynsham: Clive Farrow)

Merritt, R & Kaufman, JB (1993)
Walt in Wonderland: The Silent Films of Walt Disney
(Baltimore & Maryland: John Hopkins University Press)

Sandler, K (ed) (1998)
Reading the Rabbit: Explorations in Warner Bros. Animation
(New Brunswick: Rutgers University Press)

Sigall, M (2005)
Living Life Inside the Lines
(Jackson: University of Mississippi Press)

ART AND ANIMATION

Allan, R (1999)
Walt Disney and Europe
(London: John Libbey)

Faber, L & Walters, H (2004)
Animation Unlimited: Innovative Short Films Since 1940
(London: Laurence King Publishing)

Finch, C (1988)
The Art of Walt Disney: From Mickey Mouse to Magic Kingdoms
(New York: Portland House)

Gravett, P (2004)
Manga: Sixty Years of Japanese Comics
(London: Laurence King Publishing)

Jones, C (1990)
Chuck Amuck
(London: Simon & Schuster)

Jones, C (1996)
Chuck Reducks
(New York: Time Warner)

McCarthy, H (2002)
Hayao Miyazaki: Master of Japanese Animation
(Berkeley, California: Stone Bridge Press)

Pointon, M (ed) (1995)
Art History
[Cartoon: Caricature: Animation], Vol 18 No 1, March 1995

Russett, R & Starr, C (1988)
Experimental Animation: Origins of a New Art
(New York: Da Capo)

Wells, P (1997) (ed)
Art and Animation
(London: Academy Group/ John Wiley)

Wiedemann, J (ed) (2005)
Animation Now!
(London & Los Angeles: Taschen)

Withrow, S (2003)
Toon Art: The Graphic Art Of Digital Cartooning
(Lewes: Ilex)

ANIMATION STUDIES

Bell, E et al (eds) (1995)
From Mouse to Mermaid: The Politics of Film, Gender and Culture
(Bloomington & Indianapolis: Indiana University Press)

Brophy, P (ed) (1994)
Kaboom!: Explosive Animation from America and Japan
(Sydney: Museum of Contemporary Art)

Bryman, A (1995)
Disney and His Worlds
(London & New York: Routledge)

Buchan, S (ed) (2006)
Animated 'Worlds'
(Eastleigh: John Libbey)

Byrne, E & McQuillan, M (1999)
Deconstructing Disney
(London & Sterling: Pluto Press)

Canemaker, J (ed) (1988)
Storytelling in Animation
(London: Samuel French)

Cook, B & Thomas, G (2006)
The Animate! Book: Rethinking Animation
(London: Lux)

Cholodenko, A (Ed) (1991)
The Illusion of Life
(Sydney: Power/AFC)

Cholodenko, A (Ed) (2006)
The Illusion of Life II
(Sydney: Power/AFC)

Cohen, K (1997)
Forbidden Animation
(Jefferson, North Carolina & London: McFarland & Co)

Furniss, M (1998)
Art in Motion: Animation Aesthetics
(London & Montrouge: John Libbey)

Gehman, C & Reinke, S (eds)
The Sharpest Point: Animation at the End of Cinema
(Ottawa: YYZ Books)

Giroux, H [1999]
**The Mouse that Roared: Disney
and the End of Innocence**
[Lanham & Boulder: Rowman &
Littlefield Publishers Inc]
—

Goldmark, D [2005]
**Tunes for Toons: Music
and the Hollywood Cartoon**
[Berkeley & Los Angeles:
University of California
Press]
—

Hames, P [ed] [1995]
**Dark Alchemy: Films of
Jan Svankmajer**
[Oxford: Greenwood Press]
—

Hendershot, H [ed] [2004]
Nickelodeon Nation
[New York & London: New
York University Press]
—

Kanfer, S [1997]
**Serious Business: The Art
and Commerce of Animation
in America from Betty Boop
to Toy Story**
[New York: Scribner]
—

Klein, N [1993]
**Seven Minutes: The Life and
Death of the American Cartoon**
[New York: Verso]
—

Lehmann, C [2006]
**American Animated Cartoons
of the Vietnam Era**
[Jefferson, North Carolina
and London: McFarland &
Company Inc. Publishers]
—

Lent, J [ed] [2001]
**Animation in Asia and
the Pacific**
[Bloomington: Indiana
University Press]
—

Leslie, E [2002]
**Hollywood Flatlands:
Animation, Critical Theory
and the Avant-Garde**
[London & New York: Verso]
—

Levi, A [1996]
**Samurai from Outer Space:
Understanding Japanese
Animation**
[Chicago & La Salle:
Open Court/Carus]

Leyda, J [ed] [1988]
Eisenstein on Disney
[London: Methuen]
—

Midhat, A [2004]
Animation and Realism
[Zagreb: Croatian Film
Club Assoc]
—

Napier, S [2001]
**Anime: From Akira to
Princess Mononoke**
[New York: Palgrave]
—

Patten, F [2004]
Watching Anime, Reading Manga
[Berkeley, California:
Stone Bridge Press]
—

Peary, G & Peary, D [eds]
[1980]
The American Animated Cartoon
[New York: Plume]
—

Pilling, J [ed] [1984]
**That's Not All Folks: A
Primer in Cartoonal Knowledge**
[London: BFI]
—

Pilling, J [ed] [1992]
**Women and Animation:
A Compendium**
[London: BFI]
—

Pilling, J [ed] [1997]
A Reader In Animation Studies
[London: John Libbey]
—

Robinson, C [2005]
Unsung Heroes of Animation
[Eastleigh: John Libbey]
—

Sobchak, V [2000]
**Meta-morphing: Visual
Transformation and the
Culture of Quick Change**
[Minneapolis & London:
University of Minneapolis
Press]
—

Smoodin, E [1993]
**Animating Culture: Hollywood
Cartoons from the Sound Era**
[New Jersey: Rutgers
University Press]
—

Smoodin, E [ed] [1994]
**Disney Discourse: Producing
the Magic Kingdom**
[London & New York:
Routledge/AFI]

Stabile, C & Harrison, M
[eds] [2003]
Prime Time Animation
[London & New York:
Routledge]
—

Wasko, J [2001]
Understanding Disney
[Cambridge & Malden:
Polity Press]
—

Watts, S [1997]
**The Magic Kingdom:
Walt Disney and the
American Way of Life**
[New York: Houghton Mifflin]
—

Wells, P [1996]
Around the World in Animation
[London: BFI/MOMI Education]
—

Wells, P [1998]
Understanding Animation
[London & New York:
Routledge]
—

Wells, P [2001]
'Art of the Impossible'
from G. Andrew [ed],
Film: The Critics' Choice
[Lewes: Ivy Press]
pp 308-339
—

Wells, P [2002]
Animation and America,
[Edinburgh: Edinburgh
University Press]
—

Wells, P [2002]
**Animation: Genre
and Authorship**
[London: Wallflower Press]

ANIMATION PRACTICE
—

Blair, P [1995]
Cartoon Animation
[Laguna Hills, Ca: Walter
Foster Publishing]
—

Beckerman, H [2004]
Animation: The Whole Story
[New York: Allworth Press]
—

Birn, J [2000]
**Digital Lighting
and Rendering**
[Berkeley, Ca:
New Riders Press]

Corsaro, S & Parrott, CJ
[2004]
**Hollywood 2D Digital
Animation**
[New York: Thomson
Delmar Learning]
—

Culhane, S [1988]
**Animation: From Script
to Screen**
[London: Saint Martin's
Press]
—

Demers, O [2001]
**Digital Texturing
and Painting**
[Berkeley, Ca:
New Riders Press]
—

Gardner, G [2001]
**Gardner's Storyboard
Sketchbook**
[Washington, New York &
London: GGC Publishing]
—

Gardner, G [2002]
**Computer Graphics and
Animation: History, Careers,
Expert Advice**
[Washington, New York &
London: GGC Publishing]
—

Hart, C [1997]
How to Draw Animation
[New York: Watson-Guptill
Publications]
—

Hooks, E [2000]
**Acting for Animators:
A Complete Guide to
Performance Animation**
[Oxford: Greenwood Press]
—

Horton, A [1998]
**Laughing Out Loud: Writing
the Comedy-Centered
Screenplay**
[Los Angeles: University
of California Press]
—

Johnson, O & Thomas, F
[1981]
The Illusion of Life
[New York: Abbeville Press]
—

Kerlow, IV [2003]
**The Art of 3D: Computer
Animation and Effects**
[New York: John Wiley & Sons]

Appendix

Conclusion
Bibliography
Further resources and webography
Index
Acknowledgements and picture credits

186/187

Kuperberg, M (2001)
A Guide to Computer Animation
(Boston & Oxford:
Focal Press)
—

Laybourne, K (1998)
The Animation Book
(Vancouver: Crown
Publications)
—

Lord, P & Sibley, B (1999)
**Cracking Animation: The
Aardman Book of 3D Animation**
(London: Thames & Hudson)
—

McKee, R (1999)
**Story: Substance, Structure,
Style and the Principles of
Screenwriting**
(London: Methuen)
—

Meglin, N (2001)
Humourous Illustration
(New York: Watson-Guptill
Publications)
—

Milic, L & McConville, Y
(2006)
**The Animation Producer's
Handbook**
(Maidenhead: OUP/McGraw Hill)
—

Missal, S (2004)
**Exploring Drawing For
Animation**
(New York: Thomson
Delmar Learning)
—

Neuwirth, A (2003)
**Makin' Toons: Inside the
Most Popular Animated TV
Shows & Movies**
(New York: Allworth Press)
—

Patmore, C (2003)
The Complete Animation Course
(London: Thames & Hudson)
—

Pilling, J (2001)
2D and Beyond
(Hove & Crans-Pres-Celigny:
RotoVision)

Ratner, P (2003)
**3D Human Modelling
and Animation**
(New York: John
Wiley & Sons)
—

Ratner, P (2004)
Mastering 3D Animation
(New York: Watson-Guptill)
—

Roberts, S (2004)
Character Animation in 3D
(Boston & Oxford:
Focal Press)
—

Scott, J (2003)
How to Write for Animation
(Woodstock & New York:
Overlook Press)
—

Segar, L (1990)
**Creating Unforgettable
Characters**
(New York: Henry Holt & Co)
—

Shaw, S (2003)
**Stop Motion: Craft Skills
for Model Animation**
(Boston & Oxford:
Focal Press)
—

Simon, M (2000)
Storyboards: Motion in Art
(Boston & Oxford: Focal
Press)
—

Simon, M (2003)
**Producing Independent 2D
Character Animation**
(Boston & Oxford:
Focal Press)
—

Subotnick, S (2003)
**Animation in the Home
Digital Studio**
(Boston & Oxford:
Running PR)
—

Taylor, R (1996)
**Encyclopaedia of
Animation Techniques**
(Boston & Oxford:
Focal Press)

Tumminello, W (2003)
Exploring Storyboarding
(Boston & Oxford:
Focal Press)
—

Webber, M (2000)
**Gardner's Guide to Animation
Scriptwriting**
(Washington, New York &
London: GGC Publishing)
—

Webber, M (2002)
**Gardner's Guide to Feature
Animation Writing**
(Washington, New York &
London: GGC Publishing)
—

Wells, P (2007)
**Basics Animation:
Scriptwriting**
(Lausanne & Worthing:
AVA Publishing)
—

Whitaker, H & Halas, J
(1981)
Timing for Animation
(Boston & Oxford:
Focal Press)
—

White, T (1999)
The Animator's Workbook
(New York: Watson-Guptill
Publications)
—

Williams, R (2001)
The Animator's Survival Kit
(London & Boston: Faber
& Faber)
—

Winder, C & Dowlatabadi, Z
(2001)
Producing Animation
(Boston & Oxford:
Focal Press)

ANIMATION REFERENCE
—

Clements, J & McCarthy, H
(2001)
**The Anime Encyclopaedia:
A Guide to Japanese
Animation Since 1917**
(Berkeley, California:
Stone Bridge Press)
—

Edera, B (1977)
**Full Length Animated
Feature Films**
(London & New York:
Focal Press)
—

Grant, J (2001)
Masters of Animation
(New York: Watson-Guptill)
—

Halas, J (1987)
Masters of Animation
(London: BBC Books)
—

Hoffer, T (1981)
Animation: A Reference Guide
(Westport: Greenwood)
—

McCarthy, H (1993)
**Anime!: A Beginner's Guide
to Japanese Animation**
(London: Titan)
—

McCarthy, H (1996)
The Anime Movie Guide
(London: Titan)
—

McCarthy, H & Clements, J
(1998)
The Erotic Anime Movie Guide
(London: Titan)
—

—

Students can also consult the
Animation Journal, Animation,
American Cinematographer,
Sight & Sound and Screen and
Film History for relevant
articles. There are also
other titles purely dedicated
to feature films and studio
output, which may also prove
useful. Don't forget that
books on comedy often have
some information on cartoons
as well. Similarly readers of
essays about television often
have animation-related
discussions.

FURTHER RESOURCES AND WEBOGRAPHY

—

RECOMMENDED WEBSITES

—

www.awn.com
Animation World Network

—

www.toonhub.com
Animation Resources

—

http://memory.loc.gov/ammem/
oahtml/oahome.html
Origins of American Animation

—

www.nfb.ca
National Film Board
of Canada

—

www.toonarific.com
US Animated Cartoons
Reference

—

www.toonhound.com
UK Animated Cartoons
Reference

—

http://forum.bcdb.com/
Cartoon News and Discussion

—

—

Many of the suggested
websites also have lists
of links for all aspects
of animation from practice
tutorials to festivals
to archives to research
and study.

PERSONAL WEBSITES OF FEATURED ARTISTS

—

www.lumen.nu/rekveld/wp
/index.php
Joost Rekveld

—

www.myrectumisnotagrave.com
Steve Reinke

—

www.bitterfilms.com
Don Hertzfeldt

—

www.guitarshredshow.com
Mika Tyyskä

—

www.brianevans.net
Brian Evans

—

www.EatPES.com
PES

—

www.portapak.be
Anouk de Clerq

—

www.pierrehebert.com
Pierre Hébert

—

www.easystreet.com/~joanna
www.primopix.com/goody.swf
Joanna Priestley

—

www.ericdyer.com
Eric Dyer

—

www.tscherkassky.at
Peter Tscherkassky

—

www.beeworld.net.au
Alex and Dave Beasley

—

www.gregorybarsamian.com
Gregory Barsamian

www.salier.info
www.strikebackfilms.com
Edouard Salier

—

www.thyes.com
Myriam Thyes

—

www.gravitytrap.com
www.flightphase.com
Karolina Sobecka

—

www.rosebond.net
Rose Bond

—

www.mjstpfilms.com
Marie-Josée Saint-Pierre

—

www.yhchang.com
Young-Hae Chang Heavy
Industries

—

www.littleairplane.com
Jennifer Oxley

—

www.mutanthouse.com
Youngwoong Jang

—

www.kerrydrumm.com
Kerry Drumm

—

www.johnnyhardstaff.com
Johnny Hardstaff

—

www.aslemeur.free.fr
Anne-Sarah Le Meur

OTHER SITES OF INTEREST

—

www.hoogerbrugge.com
Han Hoogerbrugge

—

www.sandanimation.com
Ferenc Cako

—

www.faultyoptic.co.uk
Faulty Optic

—

www.onedotzero.com
Onedotzero

—

www.labs.live.com
Seadragon

—

www.nitmesh.typepad.com
Photosynthing

—

www.technologicalreview.com
Multi-user interfaces

—

www.leemcewan.com
Animated social interaction

—

www.awn.com
Animation World Network

Appendix   Conclusion
                  Bibliography
                  Further resources and webography
                  Index
                  Acknowledgements and picture credits

188/189

INDEX

Appendix

Conclusion
Bibliography
Further resources and webography
Index
Acknowledgements and picture credits

190/191

ACKNOWLEDGE[...]
AND PICTURE [...]

DATE DUE

DEC. 1 8 2009

APR 2 1 REC'D

MAY 0 4 2012

APR 2 9 REC'D

Demco, Inc. 38-293

I would like to thank
Brian Morris, Renee Last,
Caroline Walmsley and Lucy
Tipton at AVA Publishing for
keeping the show on the road
in the face of all odds.
Thank you to Emmi Salonen
for the beautiful design
of the book.

Thanks too to colleagues
at the Animation Academy,
Loughborough University
School of Art and Design;
Rose Bond, for our Portland
Panel; Darryl Clifton, for
'Object React'; Jeff
Hill/Persepolis; Gareth
Howell/LUSAD; Institute of
Contemporary Arts; Magali
Montet/Persepolis; Tamás
Mundrucz/SandAnimation;
Onedotzero; Jan Peacock;
Mette Peters/Netherlands
Institute for Animation Film;
Sarah Phelps/PES Films;
Kathryn Rawson/Head Gear
Animation; Carina
Sayles/Sayles & Winnikoff
Communications; Josh
Selig/Little Airplane
Productions; Scott Surdez;
Eric van Drunen; Shane
Walters; Heather
Tilert/Little Airplane
Productions; Sue Tongue/
Faulty Optic; Victoria &
Albert Museum; Bruce Wands.

And a final huge thank you,
of course, to all the artists
represented in this book.

Cover
Courtesy of [...]

Imprint pag[...]
Courtesy of [...]
Film Board

6
Courtesy of [...]

8-9
Courtesy of [...]
Le Meur

16-17
Courtesy of [...]
Chang Heavy

19, 30-31
Courtesy of [...]

25
Courtesy of HL + HL

26-27
Courtesy of Scott Allen

28-29
Courtesy of Naor Aloni

32-33
Wonder Pets! © 2007 Viacom
International Inc. All rights
reserved. Nick Jr, Wonder
Pets! and related titles,
logos and characters are
trademarks of Viacom
International Inc

34
Pocoyo TM © Zinkia
Entertainment

35-37
Courtesy of Mika Tyyskä

40-41
Courtesy of Jonathan Cape /
Random House

43
Courtesy of Tomato

50-55
Courtesy of Selina Steward

57
Courtesy of Thorsten Ulbrich

82-83
Courtesy of Jan Peacock

87
Courtesy of Greg Barsamian

88-90
Courtesy of Joannna Priestley

97-99
Courtesy of Edouard Salier

101
Courtesy of The Moving
Picture Company

104
Courtesy of John Finnegan

105-106
Courtesy of Anouk de Clercq

107
Courtesy of the National
Film Board of Canada

108-110
Courtesy of Marie-Josée
Saint-Pierre

111-113
Courtesy of Eric Dyer

116-118
Courtesy of Joost Rekveld

0-121
[Co]urtesy of Brian Evans

2-123
[Co]urtesy of Rose Bond

9, 134-135, 137, 139
[Co]urtesy of Kerry Drumm

2
[Co]urtesy of Lydia Hawkins

3
[Co]urtesy of Kristina Hoffman

7
[Co]urtesy of Ulrika Axen
[an]d Tobias Rudquist

)-151
[Co]urtesy of Jill Kennedy

156-159
Courtesy of Peter
Tscherkassky

162-163
Courtesy of Julian Grey

166
Courtesy of Andy Huang

167
Courtesy of The Fallon Agency

168-169
Courtesy of PES

173
Courtesy of Robert Seidel

175, 177
Courtesy of Karolina Sobecka

179
Courtesy of Max Hattler

179
Courtesy of HypoSurface Corp

—

—

—

All reasonable attempts
have been made to trace,
clear and credit the
copyright holders of the
images reproduced in this
book. However, if any
credits have been
inadvertently omitted, the
publisher will endeavour
to incorporate amendments
in future editions.